SUCCESS

Miracle SUCCESS

How You Can Have It

Don Stewart

haven books
Division of Logos International
Plainfield, N.J. 07060

All Scripture references are taken from the King James Version, unless otherwise noted as TLB (The Living Bible), TAB (The Amplified Bible), Phillips, 20th Century New Testament, or Lamsa.

MIRACLE SUCCESS
Copyright © 1979 by Don Stewart Evangelical Association
All rights reserved
Printed in the United States of America
Library of Congress Catalog Number: 80-83755
International Standard Book Number: 0-88270-484-2

Haven Books
A division of Logos International
Plainfield, New Jersey 07060

"... thou shalt make thy way prosperous, and then thou shalt have good success."

(JOSH. 1:8)

Contents

Introduction: You can have something
better—even if it takes a miracle   i
     Three Keys to God's Master Plan
     How God's Master Plan has changed our
       ministry
     Why I wrote this book
     This book is for you
     Move into position for your miracle
     Five steps to miracle success

1. God's best friend was a millionaire   1
     Are you afraid of prosperity?
     Bible examples of success
     The New Testament also gives examples
     God wants to bless you too
     Testimonies from God's Master Plan
       partners
     God sent a $5,000 blessing

2. The purpose of prosperity   13
     God's Master Plan is based 100%
       on the Bible

Where do success and prosperity
come from?
Four divine sources of prosperity
Why God wants you to prosper
Your prosperity and success make God
happy
Prosperity is a positive witness
God's Master Plan to evangelize the world
The proof of the pudding is in the eating
$1,080 was unexpected, but no surprise
God is a mathematician—He multiplied
what we gave

3. **Turn your stumbling blocks into
   stepping stones**   31
   Out with the bad air, in with the good air
   Stumbling block No. 1: Money is the root of
   all evil
   Stumbling block No. 2: Wealth is worldly
   Stumbling block No. 3: Poverty is Godly
   Stumbling block No. 4: Rich men go to hell
   Stumbling block No. 5: God will overlook
   laziness
   Stumbling block No. 6: If a camel can't go
   through a needle, how can a rich man go to
   heaven?
   Stumbling block No. 7: Rich men are
   miserable, or are going to be
   Stumbling block No. 8: Poor people are rich in
   faith
   Stumbling block No. 9: Jesus taught His disciples they should not even have as much as two
   coats

Contents

Stumbling block No. 10: We're supposed to suffer with Christ if we want to reign with Him

Finding God's path to prosperity

God's Master Plan has brought us a new kind of life

4. How to live above your circumstances   53

What to when you're sick and tired of being sick and tired

There's no such thing as an accident in God's Master Plan

Doubt your doubts and believe your beliefs

Trust God, Give to Him, and Expect Something Better

Ask, seek, knock

The key to confidence is developing discipline

Jesus will come to you at the point of your need

A new way of thinking and a better life

5. Who do you think you are?   69

Breaking out of the "slave mentality"

Stop seeing poverty and start seeing prosperity

You can be the way God sees you

"God, You've got a problem"

You are unique—one of a kind

"Your Daddy's rich"

6. How to let go of loneliness   79

Loneliness has many causes and expressions

God can heal loneliness
Six suggestions to help you be set free
    1. God knows who you are
    2. Realize you are never alone
    3. Your very living is in God's fellowship
    4. Remind yourself that God's presence is everywhere
    5. Realize there are other lonely people in the world
    6. Get involved in God's work

7. Plant what you've got and harvest what you need   **87**
Receiving begins with giving
You'll get more out if you put more in
The laws of the harvest
Where should your giving go?
Don't plant posies when you need potatoes
Nothing happens until somebody gives something
Seven characteristics of sowing and reaping
Giving is the key to happiness

8. You lose what you hold onto and multiply what you give away   **99**
There's nothing worse than wormy manna
The curse of stinginess
Three rules for giving
The key to success is putting God first

9. What is that in your hand?   **109**
The rod of Moses
The rod of God
Until there is sacrifice, there is no giving

Contents

How to succeed when you've already failed

Be part of the answer instead of part of the problem

What happens when you put God first?

10. **The Kingdom keys to prosperity** **119**
    You can't beat God giving
    Nine prosperity principles you can read in your Bible
    1. Keep God's Word
    2. Believe God's man
    3. Seek the Lord
    4. Live a righteous life
    5. Be a tither
    6. Put God First
    7. Always give before you receive
    8. Give willingly and generously
    9. Believe the promises and patiently wait for their fulfillment

    "For the first time in my life I know where I'm going and what I want to do"

    "We thought there was no way out of our financial problems"

    "I'd never received a big, unexpected blessing until I started working with God's Master Plan"

11. **Sharing my secrets for success** **127**
    When you feel like you can't go on
    When you can't find true happiness
    When you need encouragement from someone who doesn't give up

When you're tired of figuring out what you're
   doing wrong
When the devil tells you you're a fool
When you pray and nothing happens and your
   faith takes a beating
When the thing that means the most to you slips
   away just when you thought you had it
When you think you'll never get well
When you lose instead of winning

12. Send *now* prosperity   **141**
  An act of obedience opens the door
  Vow and pay
  "All things are *now* ready"
  There is no tomorrow in God's Master Plan
  Send *now* prosperity
  It all depends on you

13. Bible keys for Miracle Success   **151**
  1. You were created in the image of God, filled
     with special God-like qualities
  2. You are God's miracle of success for the
     world to see
  3. God takes care of His own, and you
     are His
  4. Let God release you from anger and bitter-
     ness with His Master Key called
     forgiveness
  5. We learn success secrets from studying our
     past failures and then moving ahead
  6. Don't dwell on past failures and
     mistakes
  7. Reaching out to others in need, planting

Contents

positive seeds of love and encouragement,
will put you a step ahead

8. Loneliness and aloneness are not
the same

9. God's Master Plan for your life is beyond
what you can possibly dream

10. The road to success is always under
construction

11. God won't release you from all your problems, but He promises you success in
dealing with your problems. And He
will take you through the valley to something better

12. You can have the mind of God if you only ask
for it

13. Success in any area of life requires discipline and hard work

14. Success comes in cans, not can'ts

15. God's success for you is all inclusive

16. Don't give up!

17. Grace, God's love and favor, is a free gift to
help you on the road to success

18. Keep planting seeds. Plant what you've got
and harvest what you need

19. Ask God for guidance when an important
decision needs making

20. Do your best—and let God handle the
rest

21. Take pride in the special job God has
given you

22. Success begins with liking yourself

23. You have unlimited potential

24. You should have definite goals in mind, a plan for achieving miracle success
25. Always look up instead of letting a bad situation drag you down
26. Let God tame the fear and worry in your life. These are real barriers to achieving success
27. The truth will set you free
28. God's healing promises are for you!
29. Exercise common sense and discipline in the areas of exercise and proper eating habits
30. Courage is not the absence of fear
31. Claim miracle success in your life today because it is God's plan for you

Introduction

*You can have something better—
even if it takes a miracle*

When I wrote my first book about God's Master Plan, I tried to share everything I knew about the Bible principles of prosperity. I filled up the pages with lessons God had taught me over the years through the experiences of daily living.

That book, *How You Can Have Something Better through God's Master Plan*, literally revolutionized the lives of thousands of people across America and around the world. It had an impact far beyond anything I had expected. The first printing of 100,000 copies was gone in a matter of a few months and a second edition had to be ordered. Then the book was translated into Spanish and printed.

Thousands of copies of the *Something Better* book are still being sent out to people who want to find out about God's Master Plan and how to put it to work in their lives.

Because it really works! Within a few weeks

after the first edition of *Something Better* was released, I started getting testimonials from people who were proving the principles of God's Master Plan. I got stacks of beautiful, amazing, exciting letters from people who were receiving tremendous blessings from the hand of God.

New friends wrote to say that after they started practicing the principles of God's Master Plan, good things started happening. Some were able to pay mountains of long overdue bills. Some got new jobs. Others moved into new houses, or got new furniture. Several were able to get brand new automobiles.

But the "something better" people started enjoying was not limited to material things. Hundreds found a new spiritual depth in their lives. Many couples discovered new love and vitality in their marriages. Parents found new ways to touch and communicate with their children, and entire families got back together. Still other people found healing for every hurt of their life.

Let me tell you, it was exciting to see what God was doing through His Master Plan. Each time I read a letter or talked with someone who had a testimony to share, it was almost as if God was proving to me all over again that the lessons and principles He had revealed to me were really true.

Three Keys to God's Master Plan

I found myself changing and growing as I began using God's Master Plan to shape and direct my personal everyday activities, as well as using the "three keys" as management tools for our worldwide ministry of missionary evangelism. The three keys of God's Master Plan are, of course:

1. Trust God as your Supplier. *"My God shall supply all your need according to his riches in glory by Christ Jesus"* (Phil. 4:19).

2. Put God first—by giving. Give Him what you have so He can use it to provide what you need. *"Give, and it shall be given unto you; good measure, pressed down, and shaken together, and running over, shall men give into your bosom. For with the same measure that ye mete withal it shall be measured to you again"* (Luke 6:38).

3. Expect something better. *"What things soever ye desire, when ye pray, believe that ye receive them, and ye shall have them"* (Mark 11:24).

Just because I started patterning my life according to God's Master Plan didn't mean all my problems stopped. In fact, it almost seemed that more faith challenges than ever came along. Kathy and I found that we still had to work to keep the lines of communication open with our two children, just as all parents do.

There were times when it was difficult to make our family budget stretch to cover all our regular needs and still take care of those unexpected expenses that came along.

Since I wrote the *Something Better* book, our family has had to face the loss of a loved one (my sister's husband), work hard on our personal spiritual growth, and deal with a variety of personal crises. For example, we had a small car that needed some repairs. We spent quite a bit of time and money to have the mechanical work done on it and get it in pretty good shape. Then one day I was driving it to an appointment. I stopped in traffic, and suddenly the car caught on fire. I barely managed to jump out before the whole interior was swallowed up in flames. The car was totally destroyed in a matter of minutes—the heat was so intense that the keys I left in the ignition melted together!

Yes, our family still has problems. The difference is that now we know how to deal with them—through God's Master Plan. We constantly remind ourselves that the Lord's will for us is good—that He wants us to have something better. We look to Him as our Supplier for every need.

How God's Master Plan has changed our ministry

God's Master Plan has made some dramatic

changes in our ministry, too. The Don Stewart Evangelistic Association has come a long way since Kathy and I started out holding revival meetings in little gospel tents. I remember well when it was a major struggle to try and meet a ministry budget of a few hundred dollars a week. A few years later, when God placed the full responsibility of this worldwide ministry on my shoulders, I recall that the debts I "inherited" amounted to many thousands of dollars. It seemed an enormous burden and challenge.

Now, our prayer and soul winning outreaches stretch around the world. Our magazine is printed on three continents and distributed in several countries to thousands of homes. Our books and literature are printed and read in many countries. We hold major missionary crusades that fill giant coliseums, stadiums and fields in Mexico, South America, the Philippines, India and Africa—wherever the Lord leads us to go. We are on television each week in major cities. Our prayer ministry is in operation 24 hours a day, 365 days a year. God has given us a hard-working, dedicated staff to assist us in our headquarters offices in the United States, Canada, the United Kingdom and the Philippines.

To keep these outreaches going, I must meet financial obligations of thousands of dollars every week. There was a time when I would have thought this was impossible. But God has proven to me over and over that nothing is too hard for Him. He has taught me many new secrets for success that always produce results. I have learned how to live my personal life and carry out every part of my ministry in accordance with God's Master Plan. I find that every day is a new adventure.

Why I wrote this book

Not everybody who wrote to me after reading the *Something Better* book had a testimony to share. Some of them still needed help in understanding and applying the principles of God's Master Plan. They said, "Rev. Stewart, can you tell us more? We need a further explanation of what prosperity is, why we should have it and how we can get it."

One lady wrote, "I really want to believe God has something better for me, but I've been down so long I'm afraid to let myself hope it could really happen. I don't think I could stand being disappointed again."

A man said, "When I read what you say about God's Master Plan it makes sense and I get all excited about it. But somehow when I go out and face up to all my problems and troubles, I don't know how to make it work. Can you tell me how to 'plug into' the power of God's Master

Plan?"

Still another woman said, "I hear about all these other people getting miracles, and Lord knows I need one too. But I never seem to be at the right place at the right time. Can God's Master Plan bring a miracle down here where I live?"

As I read and prayed over these letters—and many more like them—I realized I had to write another book and try again to share the principles of prosperity and the secrets for success God has helped me discover.

Perhaps there have been times you've felt like these people. You believe in God's Master Plan, but you feel you need more help in putting its power to work in your life. If so, then. . .

This book is for you

In the pages of this book I want to tell you what the Lord has been showing me about how to make God's Master Plan work—the first time and every time. I'll share from my heart, and I'll share some "living examples" of what I'm talking about in the form of testimonies from people just like you who have been successful in solving their problems through God's Master Plan. I'll let them tell you in their own words how they caught on to God's success secrets and made them work.

Move into position for your miracle

God's Master Plan will work for you. It can't fail because it is based 100% upon the Bible. Whatever it is you need in your life—God's got plenty. You can have something better even if it takes a miracle. Needs are the building blocks for miracles—the material miracles are made of. Whenever you find a need in your life it is a signal that God has something better for you. You have only to open yourself to God and let Him pour into your life the showers of blessing you need.

Doctors tell me that before the miracle of birth can take place, the baby must move into a certain position inside the mother. Sometimes it is necessary for the doctor to help move the baby into position so it can be born.

It is possible to block ourselves off from God's miracle success power by attitude and point of view. I believe this book will help you change that and move into position for your miracle of success.

Five steps to miracle success

Let me give you some suggestions on how to use this book so you can make God's Master Plan work for you.

First, *read* the book all the way through. Don't try to remember any particular points or instructions. Don't try to memorize any rules or scripture quotations. Just read straight through and let your mind grasp the overall picture of what the book is saying.

Second, go back and *begin studying* the book one section at a time. Take one chapter or section each day. Go over it until you completely understand what it has to say. Ask yourself how this truth could apply to your situation.

Third, keep a pen or marker handy to *under-score* the sections that stand out to you as important. Don't be afraid to mark in your book—that's the way you can get the most out of each chapter. When you finish studying and underscoring a section, go back and read the sections you have highlighted. Those parts will probably help you the most.

Fourth, *look up all the scripture references* from each chapter in your own Bible. Most of them are already printed out for you in the book, but it will be helpful for you to read them in your own Bible. You'll probably want to mark them in your Bible too, so they'll stand out to you again and again in your daily devotions.

Fifth, *write to me often.* I'm not some remote author sitting in an ivory tower somewhere. I'm your friend and prayer partner. You can get in touch with me any time with a personal letter. Let me know how you're doing in your study of the book. Share the needs and problems of your life with me so I can pray with you. Tell me about the victories God gives you. I really want to help you discover how to make God's Master Plan work for you.

So follow these five simple steps and never forget—you can have the something better you need from God—even if it takes a miracle. I know you can enjoy the same success and happiness that thousands of people around the world are enjoying through God's Master Plan. So let's begin by exploring the pages of Bible history to see how riches and prosperity go hand in hand with righteousness and spiritual power.

Remember:

1. God's Master Plan is working for multiplied thousands of people around the world. It will work for you too.

2. The three keys to something better are— trust-give-expect.

3. Using God's Master Plan doesn't mean you won't have problems—but that you will be able to deal with them successfully.

4. It's time for you to move into position for your miracle through the simple rules for success in this book.

5. To get the most benefit from this book, you should read it through, study each section,

underscore important parts, look up scripture references, and write to me for prayer.

6. You can have something better—even if it takes a miracle.

God's best friend was a millionaire

Abraham was his name.

Three times he is referred to in the Bible as the "Friend of God" (James 2:23; Isa. 41:8; 2 Chron. 20:7). No one else in the Bible is called friend of God, except Lazarus, whom Jesus called His friend and raised from the dead.

But Abraham was God's friend—and he was a millionaire. The Bible says he was "very rich in cattle, in silver, and in gold" (Gen. 13:2). In fact, Abraham and his nephew, Lot, had so many flocks, herds and tents that "the land was not able to bear them, that they might dwell together: for their substance was great" (vv. 5-6).

How did Abraham get so rich? Was his wealth inherited? Was he such a skillful manager and husbandman that he earned his own fortune? Was he a shrewd and calculating businessman who drove hard bargains and concentrated on building a massive estate?

No, the Bible teaches that Abraham was blessed of God to become wealthy. In fact, God's Word teaches us that the Lord has always blessed and prospered His people. The men who accomplished great spiritual feats often were men of wealth and means. And their prosperity in no way interfered with their spirituality.

Abraham knew that God was the source of his riches and prosperity. And he made sure everyone else knew it. He refused to accept any increase or addition to his wealth from any source that would not bring glory to God.

Once the King of Sodom and some other kings were attacked by enemy forces and defeated. The raiders carried off all the goods from Sodom and Gomorrah and took many of the people captive, including Abraham's nephew, Lot. Since there was no one else to do anything about it, Abraham armed his own servants and made an army of them. That alone gives you an idea of how wealthy Abraham was—to have an army of servants. They were sent to get back Lot and the other captive people, as well as all their possessions.

And sure enough, Abraham's servants were successful in doing that. The King of Sodom came to Abraham and said, "Just give us back our people, and you can keep all the goods as your reward."

But Abraham refused to accept as much as a shoestring. He said, "I will not take from a thread even to a shoelatchet, and . . . I will not take any thing that is thine, lest thou shouldest say, I have made Abram rich" (Gen. 14:23).

Abraham valued his friendship with God. He refused to allow material riches to interfere with his fellowship. And he never stopped understanding that God was his source and supplier of all things. Nothing was allowed to weaken or destroy his testimony.

Are you afraid of prosperity?

In my dealings with people over the past two decades, I have discovered that many people are actually afraid of prosperity. They literally believe that God somehow only loves poor people and will have nothing to do with the wealthy or prosperous. They're quite sure that the Bible teaches rich men can't go to heaven. Many of them are never comfortable unless times are hard and they are struggling to make ends meet. To them, poverty is somehow a way to express piety and earn just a small amount of favor in God's sight. They would never dare look forward to a mansion in heaven—that would be too much. They go around singing about building "a cabin in the corner of Glory Land." Have you ever met anybody like that?

Maybe you've even felt guilty at times about

3

wanting to receive something better in life. You read about the wealth of Abraham and think he must have been a special case—the exception that proves the rule that to be close to God you must be close to broke.

Bible examples of success

Well, let's take a look at some of the other giants of faith in the Bible. Maybe you'll be surprised to see that many of them were also blessed with enormous wealth.

For example, have you considered God's servant, Job? He was a man that loved God and shunned evil. And he was rich. He had 7,000 sheep, 3,000 camels, 500 yokes of oxen, 500 donkeys and a great household of servants. The Bible says, "this man was the greatest of all the men of the east" (Job 1:3).

When God allowed Satan to afflict Job with horrible calamities so that all his wealth was lost, this man still was faithful to God. "The Lord gave," he said, "and the Lord hath taken away" (Job 1:21).

At the end of the Book of Job we are told that after Job's trials were over, the Lord gave Job twice as much as he had before "fourteen thousand sheep, and six thousand camels, and a thousand yoke of oxen, and a thousand she asses" (Job 42:12).

Let's look a little further in the Bible at some

other great men of God. Isaac, for example, was a great and wealthy man. "For he had possession of flocks, and possession of herds, and great store of servants: and the Philistines envied him" (Gen. 26:14).

Jacob was prosperous, for he "increased exceedingly, and had much cattle, and maidservants, and menservants, and camels, and asses" (Gen. 30:43).

Joseph became a great man after his brothers sold him into Egypt. "And Pharaoh took off his ring from his hand, and put it upon Joseph's hand, and arrayed him in vestures of fine linen, and put a gold chain about his neck; . . . and he made him ruler over all the land of Egypt" (Gen. 41:42-43).

Moses was raised in the house of Pharaoh's daughter in great wealth, and was chosen by God to become an instrument of great deliverance. And as the leader of the Israelites—even during their years of wandering—I believe he lived in the style that the leader of such a great people would live in.

David, who is described in the Bible as a man after God's own heart, became King of Israel and Judah, and was one of the most prosperous kings who ever lived. David's wealth came from his victory over Goliath. Saul had promised a great reward to the soldier who defeated the giant—"the man who killeth him, the king will enrich him with great riches, and will give him his daughter, and make his father's house free [of taxes] in Israel" (1 Sam. 17:25). Doubtless David's wealth increased over the years.

David's son, Solomon, was even wealthier. He became famous all over the known world for his immense possessions. When he was visited by the Queen of Sheba, she said the half had not been told about his wealth. This is the man who was also known for his great wisdom, and who gave us some of the most beautiful and spiritually important books of the Bible—Song of Solomon, Ecclesiastes, and Proverbs.

Hezekiah is described as having "exceeding much riches and honour . . . for God had given him substance very much" (2 Chron. 32:27, 29). Notice the Bible carefully tells where the wealth came from.

The New Testament also gives examples

We could go on and on listing prosperous men of God. For example, we know that Matthew, one of the 12 disciples, was at one time a tax collector. The Bible says he had a house where he gave a great feast for Jesus and many other people. At that point in time in the history of the Jews, to have one's own house in Jerusalem required a person to be very well off financially.

Luke was a physician and, like many of his profession, probably enjoyed a generous income.

Peter, another disciple, was a businessman—a fisherman who owned his own boats and nets and employed others.

Lazarus, the brother of Mary and Martha and the friend at whose house Jesus often stayed, was a land owner. He had a comfortable home and could afford to entertain large groups of people. Then, the fact that he was buried in a tomb when Jesus came to raise him from the dead shows that he was a man of means. The poor of his day were not buried in tombs, but in shallow graves in a donated field—or even left outside the city walls in the refuse dump.

Joseph of Arimathaea, in whose tomb Jesus was buried, was described as a wealthy merchant.

Does it sound to you, then, that the people of God have always been poor and needy—just barely scraping by? Of course not! God's Master Plan always brings something better.

Could it be just a remarkable chain of coincidences that the great men of the Bible I have listed for you here were all men of wealth and position? Of course not. And if God only loved them in spite of their possessions and would have preferred that they be poor, then why did He send prosperity into their lives? The Bible makes it clear that these men enjoyed their wealth because of the blessings of God. For example, Hezekiah was rich because "God had given him substance very much" (2 Chron. 32:29).

God wants to bless you too. "But thou shalt remember the Lord thy God: for it is he that giveth thee power to get wealth" (Deut. 8:18).
Then must we assume that God blessed and prospered these men, but has a different plan for us? Could He treat them according to one standard and us by another? I don't think so.

My Bible says, "I am the Lord. I change not" (Mal. 3:6). "Jesus Christ the same yesterday, and today, and forever" (Heb. 13:8). "God is no respecter of persons" (Acts 10:34). Do we take God at His Word—or do we doubt Him?

One thing we know for sure—God's Word is true. Every man may be a liar. Every devil may be a liar. But the Word of God is truth. Read Ps. 119:160.

And the Word of God tells me that God's Master Plan brought prosperity, wealth and riches into the lives of men of faith and righteousness down through the centuries. Men like Abraham, Job, Isaac, Jacob, Joseph, Moses, David, Matthew, Luke, Peter, and a host of others enjoyed the rich blessings of God in their lives. And that means you and I can expect something better to come to us. We can have miracle success, be happy, well and prosperous in every part of our life.

Testimonies from God's Master Plan partners

God's Master Plan is bringing these same
blessings to people here and now. Let me share
just a couple of examples of people who have
started enjoying a new measure of prosperity
through God's Master Plan recently.

A partner from the Dallas area wrote me this
powerful testimony.

I don't know how we could make it without the Lord's help through God's Master
Plan. When I started writing to you for
help, our home was up for foreclosure. We
had no money, no food and no clothing. All
our bills were behind. Neither my husband
nor I was working.

But since you showed us how to have a
better life by using God's plan to live by,
everything has changed. I praise God for
everything He's done for us. He has blessed
us with food, clothing, and financial help.
In fact, today we have $550 in the bank and
we've never had a bank account before. All
my bills are paid. We have all the food we
can use. God has even provided new clothes
and shoes for us to wear to church. I'm so
glad about all these things because they
were things I really worried about before I
began to enjoy the blessings of God's Master
Plan. We are learning to live according to
God's expectation for us.

Isn't that a great letter? My Texas partners are finding that something better means prosperity for them. And I believe this is just the beginning of good things in their life.

God sent a $5,000 blessing

Mr. and Mrs. Seeman of Portland, Oregon, say:

God's Master Plan works in all areas of life. My husband and I had two special needs. He needed healing for a serious back problem and we needed a financial miracle. I wrote and told you all about both of these problems and asked for a prayer cloth.

When the little cloth came in the mail, I put it on my husband, we prayed and believed God together and his back was healed. God gave us the financial blessing we needed too. We have really seen His hand at work changing things, working out the details of our business problem in a wonderful way.

In answer to prayer we were able to make a sale that meant a $5,000 profit for us. This was the miracle we had needed to change our situation around. We give God all the glory for it is by His hand that we have been blessed and our needs provided.

Thank you, Rev. Stewart, for standing with us in prayer—for teaching us that we can expect miracles when we have needs. Thank you for helping us grow in faith through God's Master Plan. We've never before felt so secure and calm. Through this experience and with your help we've learned to put God first in our financial dealings on a regular basis. Now we are seeing God's goodness being added to us on a regular, daily basis. What I'm talking about is future income that is guaranteed. So you see, we had to tell you about it so you can share with us in thanking God.

God wants you to be successful. He wants you to prosper in your soul, mind and body (3 John 2). He has filled the Bible with miracle success stories for you to follow. (Read Acts 19:11 and 12). Later on I want to share still more examples of modern day success stories to stir your faith and help you receive what you need from God— through His Master Plan.

Remind yourself of these important points:

1. Many of the biblical giants of faith were blessed with great prosperity.

2. The source of their wealth was God.

3. God never changes. If He blessed them, He'll bless you.

4. Other God's Master Plan partners are being blessed with prosperity; God is no respecter of persons. So you can expect success and prosperity in your life.

> *"But thou shalt
> remember the Lord thy God:
> for it is he that giveth thee
> power to get wealth."*
> (DEUT. 8:18)

2

The purpose of prosperity

I once heard a story about two slightly tipsy fellows who wandered into the public library one rainy afternoon. One of them gathered up several picture magazines to look through, and the other settled down with a thick, heavy volume. After a while the first man finished with the magazines and went over to the other, who was paging through his book in amazement.

"What're you reading?" asked the friend.

"This here's a book called *Dictionary* by a guy named Webster," was the reply. "It ain't got much of a plot, but I've never seen a writer that had such a big vocabulary."

Obviously it is ridiculous to try and read the dictionary like a book, but in the few years I've been talking about God's Master Plan, I've come across a great number of people who needed to refer to Webster's work a little more often. Many of them seemed to have some mistaken ideas about the definitions of words like *successful* and *prosperous*. According to them, those words mean unspiritual, worldly, ungodly, sometimes even wicked and evil.

So before we go any further in this book, let's try to clear up this matter so you and I will have the same understanding when we use these words. You may want to look them up for yourself in your own dictionary. I think you'll find something like this:

> **success,** The satisfactory accomplishment of something attempted; the attainment of wealth, position, or the like; a thing or person that is successful.

> **prosper,** To be successful, especially to gain in wealth; to turn out successfully, to thrive.

Do these definitions agree with what you thought the words meant? Or are you one of the people who felt there was something bad or negative about success and prosperity? Have you ever felt guilty about desiring these things because you somehow believed they were displeasing to God?

To ever be able to make God's Master Plan work for you, you must believe that God wants you to be successful and prosperous. That is not difficult to do if you are willing to accept what God says in His Word, the Holy Bible. Very early in the Old Testament it is established that success and prosperity are part of God's will for His people.

God's Master Plan is based 100% on the Bible

Josh. 1:7-8 says:

Only be thou strong and very courageous, that thou mayest observe to do according to all the law, which Moses my servant commanded thee: turn not from it to the right hand or to the left, that thou mayest prosper whithersoever thou goest. This book of the law shall not depart out of thy mouth; but thou shalt meditate therein day and night, that thou mayest observe to do according to all that is written therein: for then thou shalt make thy way prosperous, and then thou shalt have good success.

There is no mistaking what the Bible says. These verses establish in no uncertain terms that God wants you to prosper wherever you go and to have good success. So you either believe the Word of God, or you don't.

The only place in the entire Bible where the word *success* is used is in this verse where God says you shall have it. He even gives you His opinion of it by saying it is good! And just to be sure you get the message about prosperity, He mentions it twice. He says you will "prosper whithersoever thou goest" and "thou shalt make thy way prosperous."

Where do success and prosperity come from?

Now that you understand what success and prosperity really mean, and that they are part of God's Master Plan for your life, you may be wondering how to have them. You probably want to know where prosperity comes from.

The Bible teaches that all prosperity comes from God, either directly or indirectly. Jesus said that God blesses both the evil and good with the sun and the rain. When men discover wealth from the rich deposits in the earth, they have only found what God has placed there. He is the Great Supplier, "The silver is mine, and the gold is mine, saith the Lord of hosts" (Hag. 2:8).

"Both riches and honor come of thee, and thou reignest over all; and in thine hand is power and might; and in thine hand it is to make great, and to give strength unto all" (1 Chron. 29:12).

Men may achieve success by earned prosperity, inherited prosperity, given or found prosperity, or God-given prosperity. But the ultimate source of all these blessings is God.

Four divine sources of prosperity

For the believer, there are four major ways God blesses us with success, or four divine sources of prosperity.

The first is **unlimited blessings** from God. "And all these blessings shall come on thee, and overtake thee" (Deut. 28:2). There are times when God chooses to send blessings flowing to you like a mighty river. Good things happen everywhere you turn. Everything you touch flourishes. Something better catches up to you on every road you take. The Bible says God is "able to do exceeding abundantly above all that we ask or think" (Eph. 3:20).

I don't understand everything about God's unlimited blessings. But I don't have to understand them to enjoy and appreciate them. I know they are part of God's Master Plan, and I claim the promise—"The Lord shall command the blessing upon thee" (Deut. 28:8).

The second divine source of prosperity is God blessing **the work of your hands.** "The Lord shall open unto thee his good treasure, the heaven to give the rain unto thy land in his season, and to bless all the work of thine hand" (Deut. 28:12).

God is interested in what you do. He is glad when His children find honest, worthwhile occupations. And He will bless the work you do with your hands, your skill and ability on the job, your daily business projects. When God opens His hand to you and blesses the work of your hands, then everything you do will prosper.

Have you noticed people who seem to make an effort but fail to get God's blessing upon their hands? They can work two or three jobs at a time and still never get ahead. The more they work, the deeper in debt they get. They are constantly plagued with bill collectors. Their lives are filled with misfortune and adversity.

Contrast this with the man or woman who has God's blessings on all they set their hands to. Everything they do prospers. Their needs are always met with plenty to spare. When they buy a house or invest in land, it increases in value. Their gardens flourish. Their stock increases abundantly. And, everyone can recognize the hand of the Lord upon their children.

Through God's Master Plan, you can have God's blessing on your hands so that everything you touch will increase.

The third way God enables you to become successful is by giving you **power to get wealth.** "But thou shalt remember the Lord thy God: for it is he that giveth thee power to get wealth" (Deut. 8:18).

God is saying He will give you the wisdom and knowledge to gain wealth. He will give you the ability to make wise choices and intelligent decisions. He will give you a successful, alert mind so you will readily detect manipulation in business dealings that would defraud you. He will help you understand intricate business matters, to recognize inferior values, to know the difference in good and bad ventures. And through the power of God, you will find yourself at the right place at the right time to take advantage of the opportunities to prosper and get wealth.

The fourth divine source of prosperity is **the gift of God.** "Every man also to whom God hath given riches and wealth, and hath given him power to eat thereof, and to take his portion and to rejoice in his labour; this is the gift of God" (Eccles. 5:19).

A gift is unmerited favor bestowed upon someone. The Bible shows us that God freely gives riches and wealth to His people, and gives them the power to use those resources. Many times people who work and struggle on their own to accumulate wealth never enjoy it. By the time they have their fortune, they are too old or sick to benefit from it.

You see, it doesn't do you any good to have a table just loaded down with delicious food if you're too weak and sick to eat it. It's completely futile to accumulate many possessions if you ruin your health getting them and spend the rest of your life trying to get well. What does it profit you to be a millionaire if you never have the joy of sharing your money and seeing the good it can do?

God says that when He gives you the gift of prosperity, you can rejoice and have a good

time at your work. That really means a lot.
First, it means we should work. There is something about doing a job and seeing something
accomplished that is good for a person. Work
itself is fulfilling and enriching. Working and
providing for oneself and one's family is tremen-
dously satisfying.

Second, I believe you should enjoy the kind of
work you do—be happy with the job you have.
Some people enjoy being outdoors, and they
wouldn't like a job that kept them inside all the
time. Some people like to move around, and
wouldn't enjoy a job that confined them to one
place. If you aren't happy with the job you have
now, God can give you a better one. He can help
you find a position that uses your particular
skills, or puts you with people you like, or offers
you a chance to advance and be promoted.
Liking your job helps make it possible for you to
rejoice in your labor.

Third, you can take joy in your work even if
you don't have an ideal job—even if it doesn't
pay as much as you'd like it to. Maybe you're
thinking, "I'll sure never get riches and wealth
from my job." But don't forget—your job is not
your source of supply, God is. The income you
earn, however small, can provide you with the
seed to sow that God can bless and increase. As
you give God what you have, He will bless it and
multiply it back to you many times over. You

may never *earn* a fortune, but you can be happy knowing you can have riches and wealth just the same—as a gift from God.

Why God wants you to prosper

By now you have a clear understanding of *what* prosperity is, and *where* it comes from. So let's look at the next important question that may be on your mind—*why* you should prosper. For many people this is the hardest question of all to answer satisfactorily. I remember one lady I talked with who was really struggling to understand God's purpose for prosperity.

"I've heard you talk about God's Master Plan," the woman said to me. "You say over and over that God wants to give me something better—that He wants me to be filled with His Spirit, blessed with health and healing, and to enjoy abundant prosperity. Well, that may be true for some people, but I believe God wants me to be poor and humble for His glory."

"Is that right?" I asked.

"Yes, it is," she said. "God wants me to be poor so I'll be a better witness and do more for the Kingdom of Heaven."

"Then tell me, how has being poor helped you be a better witness? Has it given you more opportunities to reach more people?"

"Well, not that I know of—not yet."

"Has it made you more influential so that

people are willing to pay attention to what you
have to say?"

"No, I can't say that it has."

"Has being poor made it possible for you to go
share the gospel with people who are unsaved?
Have you been able to give more to ministries
that are really getting the job done?"

"No, of course not," she said. "I'm so poor I'm
barely getting by myself. I have precious little
to give away."

"Then how is your being poor bringing glory
to God?" I asked. "How can you say God wants
you to be poor and needy?"

The lady was quiet for a long moment. She
sat with her head down, thinking. When she
looked up, her eyes were flashing and I could
see she wasn't through yet. "What makes you
think prosperity is so important?" she demanded.
"Why do you think God wants me to prosper?"

I looked at her and smiled. "I thought you'd
never ask," I said. And I began to share with
her the exciting Bible truths I'm going to share
with you now. I want you to know *why* God wants
you to prosper. I want you to understand the
purpose of prosperity in God's Master Plan.

Your prosperity and success make God happy

God loves you. He really does. Jesus taught
that God is like a father who wants the best for
his children. And what man, if his son asks for

bread, gives him a rock instead? Or if he asks for fish, gives him a snake? Jesus said, "If ye then, being evil, know how to give good gifts unto your children, how much more shall your Father which is in heaven give good things to them that ask him?" (Matt. 7:11). God loves you and He has something better for you.

Think for a minute. When your sons and daughters go out in the world on their own, would it make you happy or bring glory to you if they just scraped along and barely got by? Someone says, "Who is that poor guy over there—he's about to starve to death, he looks sick and run down, and he's all depressed and sad?"

And someone answers, "Oh, that's the Jones boy—he's living that way to bring glory to his folks."

You say, "But that makes it sound ridiculous!"

That's because it is ridiculous to think that our poverty can in some way bring glory to God, the King of Heaven. Just the opposite is true. My Bible says, "The Lord . . . hath pleasure in the prosperity of his servant" (Ps. 35:27). That means when good things come your way and you get all excited and thrilled about it, God is looking on and He's smiling. It makes God happy to see you enjoying the blessings He sends to you.

Look at this—"It is your Father's good pleasure

to give you the kingdom" (Luke 12:32). God loves to give—He takes pleasure in providing all the good things you need. So why not make God happy? Give Him a chance to bless you.

Prosperity is a positive witness

God wants you to prosper and be successful so you will have more influence in witnessing about the goodness of God. Tell me this. When a manufacturer puts someone on television to endorse his product, does he pick a winner or a loser? Does he use Fred the failure or Sam the success?

If you wanted to attract lots of attention to a public testimony for the Christian way of life, would you announce as your speaker, Norris Nobody or Phillip Famous?

Now I'm not saying you have to be rich or famous to accomplish anything for God. But I am saying that a testimony that Christ is the answer to all life's problems is more convincing when it comes from someone who looks as if he has found some of those answers.

Solomon, the wisest man, who is also known as the "preacher," tells an interesting story in Eccles. 9. It seems there was a small city that was attacked by a powerful king. The army completely surrounded the city, and it appeared everyone inside the walls would be lost. But there was a "poor wise man" who lived there, and by his wisdom, he figured a way to defeat the army and save the city. After it was all over and everyone was safe, Solomon said no one remembered that same poor man. He said, "the poor man's wisdom is despised, and his words are not heard" (Eccles. 9:16).

Perhaps you're saying, "But that's not right—it shouldn't be that way." That's really not the point, is it? Solomon was simply reporting what human nature is like—pointing out the facts of life. And the truth is, prosperity is more convincing than poverty. Success is more convincing than failure. In this, then, "the children of this world are in their generation wiser than the children of light" (Luke 16:8).

So let me say it again—God has something better for you. He wants you to prosper and to become more effective as a witness of His goodness and love.

As a prosperous Christian, you can say with absolute conviction, "I know what it's like to be poor and needy and then have God supply all my needs. The Lord has saved me, healed me, prospered me—He has touched me and healed me everywhere I hurt." That is a testimony the world will pay attention to. And that is why God wants to prosper you. It's part of the divine genius of God's Master Plan.

God's Master Plan to evangelize the world

One of the main reasons God wants to see His

children successful and prosperous is to make it possible for them to help finance the evangelization of the world. That's right—prosperous Christians can do much more to help preach the gospel around the world than poor Christians can.

I'm very well aware that God owns everything in the world—all the land, cattle, silver and gold. And He certainly has the power to carry out any of His purposes through miracles, if need be. But in this world God has chosen to have the Great Commission carried out by people like you and me. The resources available to the cause of world evangelism are the ones you and I provide. So as we prosper, we are better able to finance God's work. It's that simple.

Paul the Apostle wrote, "The more you are enriched by God, the more scope will there be for generous giving, and your gifts, administered through us, will mean that many will thank God" (2 Cor. 9:11, Phillips).

I'm firmly convinced that many people have failed to allow God's Master Plan to be fulfilled in their lives because they didn't understand *why* God wanted them to prosper. The devil sometimes tries to make people believe that money is bad—that prosperity destroys spirituality. But this is just another of his lying tricks to try and defeat the plan of God. When we understand what true prosperity is and what the Christian motive for desiring prosperity should be, then we can defeat the devil.

The proof of the pudding is in the eating

Well, we've done a lot of talking about success and prosperity. We've discussed what prosperity is, where it comes from and what it's for. And I sincerely hope you've been convinced that what I've told you is true. But the real test of all this is—*will it work in your life?* Like the old saying, "The proof of the pudding is in the eating."

I challenge you to give God a chance to bless you with success and prosperity. Be willing to try God's Master Plan. It only takes a small step of faith. There are three keys—three basic steps. First, *Trust God as your Supplier*—"God shall supply all your need" (Phil. 4:19). Second, *Put God first—by giving*—"Give, and it shall be given unto you" (Luke 6:38). And third, *Expect something better*—"Believe that ye receive them, and ye shall have them" (Mark 11:24).

I know God's Master Plan will work for you. But don't just take my word for it. Read these tremendous testimonies from partners who have put it to the test and are now enjoying the benefits.

$1,080 was unexpected, but no surprise

Dear Rev. Stewart,

This afternoon I got your letter about how you'd prayed and felt that a financial miracle was on the way for me. And guess what—the next letter I opened was a check for $1,080.00. This money was completely unexpected. But I can't really be surprised because I'm a God's Master Plan member and I've been putting God first by giving every month to help you with the gospel outreaches. And I know it really works. God's been proving it to me in all the different areas of my life just like you said He would.

This financial miracle is just part of the blessing God's been putting on my family since I began with God's Master Plan. Just last week our youngest daughter, Richelle, got so sick we had to take her to the hospital. The doctors there said she had pneumonia, but she surprised everyone by recovering so fast they didn't get a chance to treat her. So Jesus is our healer and we have a great doctor with us.

But best of all the good things God's done for me and my family is that now we pray together. And we all expect the Lord to take care of what we'll need tomorrow. We feel like we really have the blessing of God upon us.

Rev. Stewart, thank you so much for telling us that there's a Master we have that cares so much and has a plan for us. I can't stop rejoicing.

Mr. and Mrs. Richard R. Tracey, Arizona

God is a mathematician—
He multiplied what we gave

Dear Rev. Stewart,

What I've been sending for God's Master Plan was from our savings. We've had a small income, but we've learned from experience that when we give what we can to help you do God's work, He multiplies it to meet the needs of the ministry and to provide for us too.

Since I've been sending in my God's Master Plan gifts, my husband got a raise and I've found work! God has really blessed us in these past few months. And do you know what? We even have money left over to put back into that savings account!

Mrs. Maria Alaniz, California

Review of highlights:
1. There is nothing negative about the defini-

tions for success and prosperity.

2. God's Master Plan is based 100% upon the Bible. And the Bible teaches in no uncertain terms that God wants you to prosper.

3. There are four divine sources of prosperity—unlimited blessings, the work of your hands, power to get wealth, and the gift of God.

4. Your prosperity is important because it makes God happy, gives you influence in witnessing, and helps you finance world evangelism.

5. People who try God's Master Plan are proving that it works in their lives. Their testimonies are proof statements.

"Both riches and
honour come of thee, and
thou reignest over all; and
in thine hand is power and
might; and in thine hand
it is to make great, and
to give strength
unto all."

(1 Chron. 29:12)

3

Turn your stumbling blocks into stepping stones

Of all the subjects frequently discussed by Christians over the years, I suppose prosperity is among the most controversial. There seem to be more misunderstandings and disagreements about financial success than almost any other topic.

Yet the Bible is very clear in its teachings about money and success. Someone has investigated and reported that one out of every five verses in the Bible deals in some way with money, wealth or possessions. Jesus devoted a great deal of time and attention to teaching His followers about stewardship. Moses in the Old Testament, and Paul in the New Testament, as well as others, had much to say about material blessings.

Still, because of mistaken interpretations and improper teachings, the Bible truths God intended to be stepping stones along the path to prosperity have become stumbling blocks to many people. In talking with friends who said

31

they had tried God's Master Plan but hadn't gotten the kind of results they'd hoped for, I discovered almost all of them were still troubled with some of these mistaken ideas.

If you're one of the people who have not been able to use God's Master Plan successfully to bring something better into your life, this chapter is especially for you. And if you have not yet put God's Master Plan to the test, the information on the next few pages can help you avoid disappointment and insure success.

Out with the bad air, in with the good air

One of the first-aid techniques used to save the lives of near-drowning victims is a form of artificial respiration. The victim is placed on his stomach and his arms spread on each side of his body. The rescuer kneels behind the stricken person's head and applies pressure on the back of the chest to force water and air out of the lungs. Then the victim's arms are pulled forward to lift the rib cage so fresh air can be pulled into the lungs. To establish the proper rhythm of pushing and pulling to restore breathing, rescuers are taught to chant, "out with the bad air, in with the good air."

Just as the water and "bad air" must be forced out of the drowning victim's lungs before "good air" can go in, some people must get rid of their mistaken ideas before they can take in the truth they so desperately wish to believe. In that sense, this chapter is going to be a kind of spiritual respirator. I'm going to try to clear up some misconceptions that may have you confused and help you turn these stumbling blocks into stepping stones.

Stumbling block No. 1: Money is the root of all evil

In the Apostle Paul's first letter to Timothy is a sentence that has been misquoted perhaps more than any other single verse I know. Paul wrote, "For the love of money is the root of all evil." (1 Tim. 6:10). But so many times people have shortened it to say that money is the root of all evil. That makes a lot of difference in the meaning.

Money is simply a means of exchange. It represents a certain amount of your time, a portion of your life itself. There was a time when a man would say, "I need a horse like the one you have. I'll work for you so many days or weeks and you can pay me by giving me that horse." Now, instead of going around and finding the people who have the things we need and trying to strike a bargain to work for them long enough to earn them, we have a medium of exchange we call money. We work for a certain number of hours to get some pieces of paper. Then we go and give some of these pieces of paper in exchange for the things we want. It's a lot more convenient for everybody that way.

To say that those pieces of paper are somehow evil in themselves is a mistake. As I've said before, money is neither good nor bad—it takes after the person who has it.

After all, money is what I use to buy food for my children. Money provides shelter for my loved ones. Money helps preach the gospel to those who have not heard. How can anyone say that money is bad—the very root of all evil?

No, the Bible says it is the *love of money* that is bad—not money itself. You see, when the pieces of paper start being more important to you than what they can do for good, something bad has happened to your thinking. When you are willing to do anything to get money, ready to compromise any principle and sacrifice your honor or integrity to possess a few dollars, the seeds of evil are growing in your life. When you start stacking up and storing pieces of paper and devoting all your time, energy and thinking to getting more pieces of paper to stack up, you're in trouble.

Let's look at what Paul had to say about this.

For men who set their hearts on being wealthy expose themselves to temptation. They fall into one of the world's traps, and lay themselves open to all sorts of silly and wicked desires, which are quite capable of utterly ruining and destroying their souls. For loving money leads to all kinds of evil, and some men in the struggle to be rich have lost their faith and caused themselves untold agonies of mind (1 Tim. 6:9-10, Phillips).

So never make the mistake of thinking that money is bad. When you think of a $100 bill, think of the good things you could do with it. With that kind of outlook, you'll never have to worry about money bringing evil to your life. It's when that $100 bill looks so good to you that you hug it up close to you and think only of storing it away so you can go look at it every now and then that you've got trouble.

Stumbling block No. 2: Wealth is worldly

I've met some people who honestly believe that to have more than one change of clothes or more than one day's food in the house is sinful. They feel that to have more than the absolute bare essentials is to have wealth. And having wealth, they are convinced, is to be worldly.

The real problem with this attitude is failing to understand the source of wealth. The Bible makes it very clear that everything under the heavens, above the heavens and in the heavens belongs to God. The psalmist wrote, "O Lord . . .

the earth is full of thy riches" (Ps. 104:24). God Himself declared, "for every beast of the forest is mine, and the cattle upon a thousand hills . . . for the world is mine, and the fulness thereof" (Ps. 50:10, 12).

And for those who only want to trust what the New Testament says, Paul repeats the message—"For the earth is the Lord's and the fulness thereof" (1 Cor. 10:26).

To make sure you understand God is talking about material wealth, my Bible says, "The silver is mine, and the gold is mine, saith the Lord of hosts" (Hag. 2:8).

Think of all the wealth of the world—gold, silver, copper, iron, lead, gases, oil, uranium, aluminum, plutonium, diamonds, coal and other minerals. Besides all this, include the fowls, the cattle and the beasts of the field, wild and tame. All the birds in the air and all the fish in the sea were made as the work of His hands or the words of His mouth.

Now are you going to tell me that all these things which God says belong to Him personally, are worldly, unspiritual and ungodly? Of course not.

Wealth is not worldly—it is of God. In fact, it is God's limitless wealth that guarantees you need never be in need. Paul said, "My God shall supply all your need *according to his riches* in glory by Christ Jesus" (Phil. 4:19).

Stumbling block No. 3: Poverty is Godly

It is amazing how many ways the devil can twist the truth to deceive people. He can take a verse of Scripture that teaches one thing and use it to confuse people into believing the exact opposite.

For example, I don't know how many times I've heard poor people say they don't want to prosper because they want to be like Jesus—that He was poor and lowly, and didn't even have a place to lay His head. But they never get around to understanding *why* Jesus was poor. The Bible says, "for your sakes he became poor, that ye through his poverty might be rich" (2 Cor. 8:9).

God is the source of abundance. He is the God of plenty, and to spare. Becoming poverty-stricken does not make you more God-like. It makes you a slave.

Take a look at Prov. 22:7—"The rich ruleth over the poor, and the borrower is servant to the lender." Did God intend for you to be a slave and a servant to others, or did He want you to be free and more than a conqueror? You've got to make up your mind about this.

Maybe this will help you—"A good man leaveth an inheritance to his children's children" (Prov. 13:22). So if you want to be Godly—if you want to be good, have enough wealth to pass on to your children and even to your grandchildren.

How are you going to do that if you live your whole life in poverty? Don't let the devil cause you to stumble over this. Climb right on top of his arguments and use them to climb higher.

Stumbling block No. 4: Rich men go to hell

Maybe you've heard teachings based on Luke 16:22-23 that poor men go to heaven and rich men go to hell. Those verses tell how a beggar named Lazarus died and was carried by the angels into Abraham's bosom. The rich man died and was buried, "And in hell he lift up his eyes, being in torments."

No one can argue the fact that, in this case, a rich man did go to hell. However, the Bible doesn't say he went to hell *because* he was rich.

But have you ever heard anyone teach on another rich and poor man team that Jesus talked about in Luke 18? A Pharisee and a publican went to the temple to pray. Now the Pharisee was an ultra-religious, super-pious man. He proudly announced that he was glad he was not like all the sinful people around him, that he fasted and paid tithes and obeyed all the laws and rituals.

The publican, on the other hand, was a businessman, a man of finance, a man of substance. You and I would probably call him rich. This man stood with his head bowed and said, "God be merciful to me a sinner."

Jesus said the rich man went to his house justified rather than the Pharisee. So you tell me—which man would have gone to heaven and which one to hell if they had died that day?

Remember all the great men of faith we discussed in the first chapter of this book. If all rich men go to hell, that would include people like Abraham, Isaac, Jacob and all the others listed there. And I firmly believe they're going to be in heaven, don't you?

So don't ever let anybody tell you that rich men are doomed to hell. It's a lie of the devil.

Stumbling block No. 5: God will overlook laziness

A stumbling block to success that is becoming an even greater problem in our day is the attitude that if we don't work and try to be productive, God will overlook our laziness and someone else will take care of us. That is a doctrine of the devil. It completely opposes all the teachings of the Bible.

Paul wrote, "This we commanded you, that if any would not work, neither should he eat" (2 Thess. 3:10).

The law of God is that poverty and want are the rewards of the slothful. "The sluggard will not plow by reason of the cold; therefore shall he beg in harvest, and have nothing" (Prov. 20:4).

"Go to the ant, thou sluggard; consider her

ways, and be wise: Which having no guide, overseer, or ruler, Provideth her meat in the summer, and gathereth her food in the harvest" (Prov. 6:6-8).

There's much more—"Yet a little sleep, a little slumber, a little folding of the hands to sleep: So shall thy poverty come as one that travelleth, and thy want as an armed man" (Prov. 6:10-11).

And Paul comments again, "He which soweth sparingly shall reap also sparingly" (2 Cor. 9:6).

Jesus told of a man who gave talents (amounts of money) to his servants and then went on a trip. One servant received five talents, and he got busy and used them to earn five more. Another servant got two talents, and he was able to earn two more. The third servant got one talent, and he didn't do anything with it, just buried it for safekeeping. Maybe he was discouraged because he didn't have as much as the other servants to work with. So he just sat down.

When the master came back, he said "well done" to the first two servants. But he called the lazy, unproductive servant wicked and slothful. Then he took away the one talent entrusted to him and gave it to the servant who had 10 (see Matt. 25).

Don't ever make the mistake of sitting around waiting for God to drop blessings and prosperity into your lap. Some people think God is like

Robin Hood—that He will take from the rich and give to the poor. But Jesus taught that God will take from the man who won't work and give it to someone who will work to multiply his assets and be profitable.

Stumbling block No. 6: If a camel can't go through a needle, how can a rich man go to heaven?

Yes, Jesus used this example in Mark 10:25. And He meant what He said. But the key to understanding this verse is knowing *which* rich men He was referring to.

Is He referring to people who have been prospered and blessed financially, to those who have houses, lands and possessions? Or is He being more specific?

If Jesus meant that people who own enough goods to be called rich will not be able to enter Heaven's gates, then we've got a serious problem with the Bible.

In Matt. 19:29, Jesus says, "Everyone that hath forsaken houses . . . for my name's sake, shall receive an hundredfold, and shall inherit everlasting life."

If owning a house would send you to hell, would Jesus give you a hundred houses? That doesn't make sense, does it? The Lord said not only would He give you back 100 times more than you give to Him, but you "shall inherit everlasting life." Now I don't know how you interpret that, but it sounds very much like heaven to me.

Then what in the world does the camel story mean? Jesus was referring specifically to the rich young ruler who had come to Him earlier asking what He had to do to be saved. Jesus told him to sell all he had and give it to the poor and to follow Him. The young man went away sorrowfully.

Now Jesus didn't want any of that young man's possessions. He wanted the young man. But because the rich young ruler loved and trusted in his wealth more than he loved and trusted God, he turned away and was lost.

Then Jesus said, "How hard it is for them that trust in riches to enter into the kingdom of God! It is easier for a camel to go through the eye of a needle" (Mark 10:24-25).

It was not riches that kept the rich young ruler out of heaven—it was *trusting in riches* rather than God. And whether you have little or much, if it is more important to you than the teachings of the Lord and the Word of God, then you might as well climb on that camel trying to wriggle through the eye of a needle.

Stumbling block No. 7: Rich men are miserable, or are going to be

It's amazing how some people can read part of

one verse—out of context—and leap to conclusions that are completely and absolutely false. This stumbling block is a perfect example. The Bible does talk about rich men howling in misery—you'll find the passage in the fifth chapter of James.

But let's read all of it to find out which rich men the apostle is talking about.

> Go to now, ye rich men, weep and howl for your miseries that shall come upon you. Your riches are corrupted, and your garments are motheaten. Your gold and silver is cankered; and the rest of them shall be a witness against you, and shall eat your flesh as it were fire. Ye have heaped treasure together for the last days. Behold, the hire of the labourers who have reaped down your fields, which is of you kept back by fraud, crieth: and the cries of them which have reaped are entered into the ears of the Lord of sabaoth. Ye have lived in pleasure on the earth, and been wanton; ye have nourished your hearts, as in a day of slaughter. Ye have condemned and killed the just; and he doth not resist you (James 5:1-6).

So what does God mean when He says, "Howl ye rich men"? He is condemning those who obtained their wealth dishonestly. These people became rich by defrauding their neighbors and by stealing. They were nothing less than criminals. Then, they used their ill-gotten gains to live in a lascivious, lewd and obscene manner. No wonder God condemned them.

But to say all rich men are condemned and will be miserable is as mistaken and unfair as to say that if one black dog bites a child, all black dogs are dangerous and should be destroyed.

Stumbling block No. 8: Poor people are rich in faith

I have heard many people teach that rich people can have no faith because the Bible teaches God has chosen the poor of the world to be rich in faith (see James 2:5). But no one has ever explained to me why, if this is true, all the poor people in the world aren't saved. Nor have the people who teach this mistaken doctrine ever made me understand how so many of the great men of faith were rich and prosperous. The Scripture did not say that faith was limited to the poor. James was teaching that congregations of believers are not to be respecters of persons. If a rich man in fine clothes with gold rings on his fingers comes in, and a poor man in threadbare clothes also comes in, the people are not to make a fuss over the one and ignore the other. God does not confine faith to any financial level. Rather, He is trying to encourage the poor to believe they too can have faith to receive God's blessings.

Stumbling block No. 9: Jesus taught His disciples they should not even have as much as two coats

That's not what Jesus taught at all. Matthew, Mark and Luke all tell the story of Jesus sending out the disciples to witness and minister. Jesus instructed them to hurry on their mission—to not take the time to earn, or provide money, food, clothing, etc. He was teaching them to trust Him for their needs. And He was teaching those to whom they ministered to provide for men of God. He said a workman was worthy of his hire—to be paid and taken care of (Luke 10:7). Jesus told His disciples that if any village or area refused to assume its responsibility, to leave it and go where the people would.

Jesus was teaching His ministers that they didn't have to earn their way before they went to preach—that God would provide for them. There was no need to carry a trunk full of supplies—God would have His people meet their needs. And I believe the disciples had a change of clothes and a new coat when they needed them.

Stumbling block No. 10: We're supposed to suffer with Christ if we want to reign with Him

This stumbling block has been around for centuries. Many people have read the verse, "If we suffer, we shall also reign with him" (2 Tim. 2:12). Then they said, "When Christ was on earth He suffered, so we must suffer too if we ever want to reign with Him." For this reason, in some countries, people afflict themselves with various kinds of torture—beating themselves with whips, carrying a cross, crawling on their hands and knees for miles—all because they want to suffer like Jesus. They feel they must make an atonement for their sins. In fact, some even go so far as having themselves crucified—actually nailed to a cross for several hours.

Of course, most "modern" believers would never go that far. But many of them do reason that since Jesus was poor, with no place to lay His head, they must be poor too. They completely overlook the biblical explanation for Jesus' poverty. "Though he was rich, yet for your sakes he became poor, that ye through his poverty might be rich" (2 Cor. 8:9).

Now, many will say that when Jesus suffered poverty that we might become rich, it was speaking of spiritual things. If this is true, when the Bible says, "Yet for your sakes he became poor," it means Jesus became *spiritually* impoverished. Can you imagine Jesus being backslidden? Of course not. We know the Lord "Was in all points tempted like as we are, yet without sin" (Heb. 4:15).

If we must be poor because Christ became poor, then we must be sick because He also "in his own body" bore our infirmities. And we must be continually sad, because He bore our sorrows. If this kind of reasoning is right, then we must also be sinful, because "he bore our sin in his own body on the tree."

But if you accept this, what do you do with verses like these? "He hath made him to be sin for us, who knew no sin; that we might be made the righteousness of God in him" (2 Cor. 5:21). "Who his own self bare our sins in his own body on the tree, that we, being dead to sins, should live unto righteousness: by whose stripes ye were healed" (1 Pet. 2:24).

When we really open our hearts and minds to God's Word, we find it teaches that Christ does not want us to suffer in body, in soul, or in the pocket book. The Scriptures declare that Christ bore our sins on the tree, bore stripes for our healing, and was poor that we through His poverty might be made rich.

What, then, do we do with 2 Tim. 2:12—"If we suffer, we shall also reign with him"? These words were written by Paul, who was referring

47

to persecution he was suffering because he was preaching the Word of God. The Bible teaches that we may have to face persecution because of our obedience to the Great Commission. But this is completely different from suffering sickness, guilt and poverty. If you suffer persecution— not poverty—you will reign with Christ.

Finding God's path to prosperity

Trying to provide answers for all the stumbling blocks people drag up could fill up a bigger book than this one, I'm sure. But by dealing with just these 10 I hope you are beginning to see how the enemy takes a partial truth and twists it into a lie. Then one mistaken belief leads to another, and pretty soon a person is so confused and defeated he doesn't know what to do.

Now, let me point you along the way to God's path to prosperity. The directions are quite simple—*Trust, Give* and *Expect.*

First, trust God as your Supplier. Believe with all your heart that He is the source of your prosperity, not the company or corporation you work for. The Bible says, "My God shall supply all your need" (Phil. 4:19). It doesn't say, your boss, your employer, the banker will supply your need. Now the Lord may use these sources as instruments to deliver what you need to you— but He is your Supplier.

By the way, if you need a raise or to move up to a better job, God is still your Supplier. Take a look at Ps. 75:6-7: "For promotion cometh neither from the east, nor from the west, nor from the south. But God is the judge."

Second, you must give if you ever want to receive. "Give, and it shall be given unto you" (Luke 6:38). Sow some seeds so you can reap a harvest. Give God something to work on—something to multiply back to you. Give Him some of the thing you need most. That's the way God's Master Plan works. And nothing happens in God's prosperity program until you give something.

Third, once you have given, expect a return. Expect something better. Get ready for a miracle. "What things soever ye desire, when ye pray, believe that ye receive them, and ye shall have them" (Mark 11:24).

And that's really all there is to it. Three simple steps that you just take over and over. And every time you take those three steps, you will find yourself farther along God's path to prosperity. Pretty soon you won't even be thinking about taking those steps—they'll just come naturally. And you'll be running full speed, not slowly inching your way along.

God's Master Plan is for you to be victorious over all the doubts, uncertainties and fears that have caused you to fail in the past. He wants you to use all your old stumbling blocks as stepping stones to something better in every part of your life.

Let me share just one testimony with you, before we go on to the next chapter, written by a lady from the Navajo Indian reservation.

God's Master Plan has brought us a new kind of life

Dear Rev. Stewart,

Let me share some good news that has happened since we joined God's Master Plan. It is really working for us. You see, my husband, Tom, has been a drunk all his life, but now he has quit drinking. A great change is taking place in his life. Then, last month we received $1,843.00 in the mail. This was unexpected—in fact, it would be impossible for me to understand if I didn't know it was the work of the Lord. It all started when we began to give and put God first. Most of our old bills are finally paid up, and we also bought some new furniture. This seems unbelievable. It just has to be God working for us to have so many good things happening to us. Thanks for your prayers and for sharing God's Master Plan with us.

Mary Smiley, New Mexico

Summary of chapter:
1. By clearing up your mistaken ideas about prosperity through a better understanding of God's Word, your former stumbling blocks can become stepping stones to success and something better.

2. The devil will try to confuse and deceive you with these stumbling blocks:
   - Money is the root of all evil
   - Wealth is worldly
   - Poverty is Godly
   - Rich men go to hell
   - God will overlook laziness
   - If a camel can't go through a needle, how can a rich man go to heaven?
   - Rich men are miserable, or are going to be
   - Poor people are rich in faith
   - Jesus taught His disciples they should not even have as much as two coats
   - We're supposed to suffer with Christ if we want to reign with Him

3. The three steps to God's path to prosperity are *trusting* (Phil. 4:19), *giving* (Luke 6:38) and *expecting* (Mark 11:24).

4

How to live above
your circumstances

Does your happiness depend upon what happens to you? Are you on the mountaintop when the sun is shining and the things that happen to you are pleasant? Then are you "down in the dumps" when the sky is gloomy and everything around you seems to be going wrong? Is your daily life like a roller coaster—an endless series of ups and downs, highs and lows?

Well I've got news for you—you don't have to live that way. God's Master Plan is not dependent upon circumstances to bring something better into your life. You can make your own weather—the shelter of God's love can keep you warm and dry against the storms of life; His showers of blessings can bring refreshing to your dry deserts of human need.

The Apostle Paul testified, "For I, however I am placed, have learnt *to be independent of circumstances*. I know how to face humble circumstances, and I know how to face prosperity. Into

all and every human experience I have been
initiated—into plenty and hunger, into prosperity and want. I can do everything in the strength
of him who makes me strong" (Phil. 4:11-13,
20th Century New Testament).

When Paul wrote the Philippian letter he
was in prison. Yet this book is often called "the
Epistle of Joy" because it is so filled with
optimism. He did not let his prison experience
rob him of his joy in the Lord.

Paul knew what it was to face poverty. He
said, "I have lived with weariness and pain and
sleepless nights. Often I have been hungry and
thirsty and have gone without food; often I have
shivered with cold, without enough clothing to
keep me warm" (2 Cor. 11:27, TLB).

It is this same Paul, though, who tells us that
poverty doesn't have to be permanent. He says,
"My God shall supply all your need according to
his riches in glory by Christ Jesus" (Phil. 4:19).
Paul knew how to let God give him something
better.

What to do when you're sick and tired of
being sick and tired

I got a letter not too long ago from a person
who had about reached the end of himself. It
seemed the harder he tried, the worse things
got. He couldn't see any light at the end of the
tunnel. There was no patch of blue anywhere in

the sky. He felt defeated and discouraged—he couldn't even remember when he *hadn't* felt that way. He summed it all up in one of the most eloquent descriptions I've ever heard. He said: *"I'm sick and tired of being sick and tired."*

Have you ever felt that way? I think all of us have been in that spot at one time or another. Perhaps it is only when we get to that place that we realize we must depend on God and follow His plan if we are to succeed.

A popular songwriter expressed it this way:
Never thought I needed help before,
Always thought I could do things by myself,
Now I know I just can't take it anymore,
With a humble heart, on bended knee, I'm
begging You, please, help me.

No sincere prayer calling out to God like this is ever refused. Sometimes the reason we get "sick and tired" is that we try to solve all life's problems by ourselves. When we realize we must depend on God and call out to Him for help, the answer always is, "Come unto me, all ye that labour and are heavy laden, and I will give you rest. I will restore health unto thee, and I will heal thee of thy wounds" (Matt. 11:28; Jer. 30:17).

There's no such thing as an accident in God's Master Plan

One reason the Apostle Paul could be independent of circumstances was because he had learned an important lesson from God. He declared, "All things work together for good to them that love God" (Rom. 8:28).

What may look like an accident has some good purpose in it or else God would not allow it to happen. The things He allows to come into our lives are part of His Master Plan for us. And they will result in something better for us—even bad things will "work for good."

Joseph's jealous brothers sold him into slavery in Egypt. But God raised him up out of prison and caused him to be promoted to second-in-command over the entire nation. A few years later Joseph could forgive his brothers and say to them, "Ye thought evil against me: but God meant it unto good" (Gen. 50:20).

I heard of a woman who visited a factory where skilled artisans were making expensive, hand-loomed rugs. She looked at a carpet and said, "That's sure not very pretty."

Her guide said, "It is one of the most beautiful carpets we have."

"But look," she protested. "There are threads going all directions, there's no design, it's just a tangled, disorderly mass of confusion."

"Ah," said the factory man, "here's the problem—you're looking at the wrong side!"

The next time you are trying to work out all your problems and everything seems to be getting more and more confused—stop before you get completely frustrated. Ask God to let you see your situation from His point of view. You may discover that what looks like a hopeless tangle from your viewpoint is part of a master plan of beautiful design from God's viewpoint.

So when you find yourself sick and tired of being sick and tired, here's what to do. Like a kitten tangled in a ball of yarn stop struggling against the circumstances that are about to defeat you. Let God heal you everywhere you hurt—in every sickness of mind, spirit, soul and body. Then rest, secure in the promises and provision of God. Once you are healed and rested, you can move past all circumstances to the something better God has for you, saying, "I can do all things through Christ which strengtheneth me" (Phil. 4:13).

Doubt your doubts and believe your beliefs

Mark Twain, the brilliant American writer who created *Tom Sawyer* and *Huckleberry Finn,* was supposedly an atheist. He is quoted as saying, "I never worry about the parts of the Bible I don't understand. . .I'm too busy worrying about the parts I do!"

That philosophy is pretty negative. But it leads us to an important secret for success. Stop worrying about the things you can't quite believe and concentrate on the things you do believe. Some Christians feel guilty when doubt comes knocking at their door. But doubt is bad only when we allow it to stop all progress in our life and never do anything to clear up those areas we're not sure of.

Some people read about the Apostle Thomas and think how terrible it was that he doubted Jesus had really risen from the dead. But I have to admire Thomas. He said, "I'll be honest—I'm not sure about this. But I want to know. I'm willing to believe. Convince me, Lord."

And Jesus simply said, "Come touch Me, Thomas, and be sure."

And that's what He says to us today—"Let Me settle your doubts. Come touch Me and be sure!"

If you have not been successful in applying God's Master Plan for success and prosperity because of certain nagging doubts in your life, I've got a secret to share that will help you now.

Doubt usually causes uncertainty, a hesitance, a slowdown—maybe even a total lack of action. Like a lost traveller at a fork in the road, the doubter stands dead still, not sure what to do or which way to go. So most of the time he doesn't do anything.

On the other hand, belief is always measured by action. Belief motivates us to go, to do, to try. What happens when a traveller believes he knows which way to go, but makes a wrong turn? He soon discovers his mistake, comes back and starts off again in the right direction. And all the while the poor old doubter is still standing there, making no progress at all.

The longer you sit trying to resolve all your doubts about success and prosperity, the longer you will fail to achieve them. "How long halt ye between two opinions?" (1 Kings 18:21).

The thing to do is doubt your doubts. What do I mean by that? Simply let any lack of action in your life be limited to your doubts themselves. Say to yourself, "I won't believe that I can't believe." Stop wrestling with your doubts— with trying to work everything out in your head before you ever get around to trying anything.

Instead, start concentrating on the things you do know, the things you do believe in. Start *doing* them.

For example, you may have doubts about how much of a reward God will bestow upon you for giving. So just don't do anything about that doubt. Wait and see if it will resolve itself. Instead, concentrate on acting upon what you do believe in—that the Word of God teaches you should give. You understand and believe that without any question. So do it. Follow the three simple keys to God's Master Plan.

Trust God, Give to Him, and Expect Something Better

Then, when God pours His blessings into

your life, you can decide for yourself whether or not God's Master Plan really works. When you begin discovering that it really does, you can wipe out those troubling doubts. You will soon discover that a person with an experience is never disturbed by the doubts of a person with just an opinion to go on.

Ask, seek, knock

Sometimes people say to me, "Rev. Stewart, it would be so much easier to put God's Master Plan to work if we just had a definite word from the Lord to tell us exactly what to do. We know about putting God first in our giving and being faithful to His work and His kingdom. But then what do we do? Do we just wait for His blessings to come, or is there something we must do to receive them?"

The answer is simple—so simple it is overlooked by too many people today. Jesus said, "Ask, and it shall be given you; seek, and ye shall find; knock, and it shall be opened unto you: For every one that asketh receiveth; and he that seeketh findeth; and to him that knocketh it shall be opened" (Matt. 7:7-8).

Notice that Jesus said when you ask it *shall* be given—not may be, could be, should be, or probably will be. It *shall* be. That is God's promise.

What happens if you don't ask? Again the

answer is simple—you don't receive. "Ye have not," writes the Apostle James, "because ye ask not" (4:2).

So put God to the test. Obey His Word. Then ask, seek, knock—reach out for something better from God. You will begin to get, to receive, to be given the things you have asked for. You will start finding what you've been seeking. The doors you've been knocking on will start swinging open. God's Master Plan will start shaping your life into what He wants you to be.

The key to confidence is developing discipline

How can you continually cope with life and live above your circumstances every day? How can you always face the morning with assurance and confidence? How can you be sure every problem and need that may arise will turn out for your good?

The key to having confidence in any area of life is discipline. There's another of those words so many people misunderstand. According to the dictionary, discipline is a state of order derived from instruction, exercise and training.

You see, human nature causes us to be uncertain, unsure, and uncomfortable when we are in a situation that is unfamiliar and confusing. But when we can see the order of things, we begin to understand them, relax, and feel secure. How do we see the order? By instruction first, then by practice.

How can an Olympic athlete appear so confident when he lines up to compete for the world championship? He is confident because he has been taught what to do, he has practiced what to do, he has trained his body and mind to react in a certain way to the challenge. He has disciplined his body, and he knows what to expect.

A public speaker stands up before a mass audience of thousands and looks unflinching into the bright lights and the television cameras. How can he speak with such naturalness and assurance? Because he has done his homework. He knows what he is expected to talk about, he has studied his subject and practiced his presentation. He knows how to get started and when to quit. He has disciplined his mind and he is confident.

How do soldiers find the courage to march into battle amidst terrible dangers and perform their assigned duties under fire? Through discipline—they have been instructed, trained and drilled until performance under pressure becomes almost second nature.

On the other hand, how does a child live happy, cheerful and confident, secure in the love of his parents and family? Through daily discipline—kindly instruction, firm exercise and regular training in what is expected of him. Show me a youngster who has an inferiority complex, is rebellious or in some other way cries out for attention and I'll show you a child who more than likely does not receive proper discipline at home.

Discipline always produces confidence. And when there is no confidence, discipline is needed somewhere!

Do you feel unsure of yourself in spiritual matters—ill at ease in the Presence of God? You need to discipline yourself by daily reading of God's Word and by spending time in prayer, talking with God.

Are you constantly suffering in your body from a variety of problems and ailments? Perhaps part of the answer is personal discipline in the areas of proper rest, diet and exercise. God never intended for us to abuse our bodies with poor care, or by polluting them with harmful substances.

And if your financial situation is a shambles— a never-ending series of emergencies and problems, how can you be confident and victorious? Again the answer may be discipline. Perhaps your budget needs overhauling. As stewards of what God gives us, we are responsible to use every resource wisely. If you have constant trouble in this part of your life, it's a pretty good indication you have not been putting God first in giving.

You may be saying, "Oh, if God will just meet my needs I'll be glad to give to Him." But that's not how it works. You've got it backwards. The Bible says, "Give, and it shall be given unto you." Discipline yourself. Obey God. Do what He says. And as surely as morning follows night, you will become confident in money matters. You won't hate to see the mailman coming. You won't hide when the doorbell rings. You won't worry about who is calling when the telephone rings. You'll know your house is in order. And you can step out in confidence—more than a conqueror!

Jesus will come to you at the point of your need

Perhaps you've always looked upon circumstances as something to be dreaded—ever present reminders of need in your life. But remember, needs are the building blocks for miracles. You must have a need if you are to receive a miracle. In fact—that is exactly where the Lord will come to you. Jesus will meet you at the point of your need.

The Bible is full of examples. One time the disciples were in a small ship that was being blown by contrary winds and tossed by the waves. My Bible says, "Jesus went unto them, walking on the sea" (Matt. 14:25). He told them not to be afraid, and He met their need by

64

calming the wind and the waves. So you see, the Lord came to them *because of* their circumstances—He came to them at the point of their need.

After the crucifixion of Christ, Mary Magdalene was crushed with grief. She who had been forgiven of so much, who had loved Christ so devotedly, now grieved so bitterly she was almost overcome. And at this critical point of her need, Jesus appears to her. He comforts her, gives her new faith, new hope and a message to share. The very circumstances of her need brought Jesus to her. (See John 20:16).

As two sorrowful disciples walked along the road to Emmaus, suddenly the Lord came and walked with them (Luke 24:15). He came to them at the point of their need. Another time when His frightened, troubled followers locked themselves in a room away from the world, Jesus came to them right through the wall. Their need compelled Him to be there (John 20:26).

So take a new look at your circumstances. Begin to see them as opportunities rather than obstacles. Even if they loom so large they almost shut out the light of day, don't be dismayed. He will come to you there at the point of your need. And He will lift you over and above your circumstances into the light of His day. This is the promise of God's Master Plan.

A new way of thinking and a better life

Let's close this chapter by sharing a beautiful letter of testimony from a partner in Buffalo, New York.

Dear Rev. Stewart,

When you first introduced me to God's Master Plan I was so troubled. I had so many needs and problems I didn't know where to turn. But the Lord used you to be such a blessing to me. I confided in you, and you wrote me letters that had just the help I needed. Now I'm so thankful for God's Master Plan because it's beginning to give me a new way of thinking and a better life. I enjoy having a part in a ministry that gives the truth to other troubled people. That's why I'm happy to send my offering to help with the work you are doing for God, and I'm grateful to have someone to share with.

In review:

1. God's Master Plan is not dependent upon circumstances to bring something better into your life.

2. Poverty doesn't have to be permanent.

3. The solution for being "sick and tired" is to stop struggling, let God heal you every-

where you hurt, rest in His promises—then
move out in His strength.

4. Act on what you do believe and watch your
   doubts resolve themselves.

5. Ask—seek—knock according to Matt. 7:7.

6. To be confident, develop discipline.

7. Look for Jesus to come to you at the point of
   your need.

> *"Ask, and it shall
> be given you; seek, and
> ye shall find; knock, and
> it shall be opened unto you:
> For every one that asketh
> receiveth; and he that
> seeketh findeth; and to
> him that knocketh it
> shall be opened."*
>
> (Matt. 7:7-8)

Who do you think you are?

It was one of the most exciting letters I've ever read. It came to me from a young lady in St. Louis, Missouri, who had recently become a partner in God's Master Plan. She had written several times before to share some of the needs of her life. I had prayed for her and answered her letters. Most of all, I had tried to encourage her to begin *trusting*, *giving* and *expecting*. So it was a special thrill to get this letter.

Dear Rev. Stewart,
   I could hardly wait to get home today so I could write and tell you what the Lord has done for me. Tonight when I went to school, one of my supervisors called me to his office and gave me a check for $100. He said the money was mine because I'd made exceptional progress in my courses. He said my attendance record, effort and attitude were being noticed.

I was so happy I almost cried. Only the Lord knew how much I needed that money. But that isn't all God has given me. He has been taking care of things ever since you helped me to understand how to put God first and trust Him to take care of what I need. Thank God for His Master Plan— because when I joined it the Lord really began sending some neat blessings to me.

You see, I decided to put God ahead of everything else by doing my God's Master Plan giving before I took care of other things. Then I did like you said and thought about what I needed most.

Now this may be different from what a lot of people tell you about—but I prayed and asked God to *help me make something out of myself. I wanted to be somebody.* And I knew I couldn't do it alone.

God answered that prayer. He made it possible for me to go to this fine business school and I'm doing fine. God helped me make good at school, and sent me the money to stay there. I've been getting a $70 check every month for going to school. It looked like I might not get to finish because the money would stop on my birthday. But as you can see, the Lord has made a way for me to stay on.

I'm going to spend this money wisely because God gave it to me by a miracle. I'll be able to buy some new clothes—something I haven't done for a long time.

God has also given me a lot of nice things— a good television set, a stereo and some other blessings, great and small. I always send in my God's Master Plan offering and I've seen that God blesses me more every time I do. I'm learning to trust the Lord because He is the only way for me. Whenever I am down I go to Jesus and tell Him my problem. He lifts the burden off my heart and makes me feel happy inside.

I don't know if this is what you mean when you talk about something better—but it's good enough for me!

Breaking out of the "slave mentality"

I'm especially glad to share this letter of testimony with you because it illustrates another important secret of success. Good things started happening to this girl soon after she decided she wanted to be somebody—when she prayed for God to make something out of her. Through God's Master Plan, she suddenly began to realize who she was—a child of God and a joint heir with Christ.

The Bible tells how the Israelites were slaves in Egypt for 400 years. They were so oppressed and put down they began to act like slaves, to think and feel like slaves. As new generations came along, they developed a slave mentality. They expected nothing but hardship. They couldn't even imagine what it would be like to be free. They never hoped to have anything, or be anybody. Day after day they waited for someone else to tell them what to do, where to go, how to live.

Even when Moses came to lead them to the Promised Land they had a hard time shaking off their slave mentality and starting to act like God's chosen people again. The Bible says, "They hearkened not unto Moses for anguish of spirit, and for cruel bondage" (Exod. 6:9).

Do you remember the story of Moses sending 12 spies into Canaan? (Num. 13). Only two of them came back to report that the land could be taken. The other ten said, "It's a land full of giants just waiting to beat up on us." Their slave mentality kept them from possessing the land flowing with milk and honey. The key to their failure is in verse 33, where they declared, "And we were in our own sight as grasshoppers."

Have you ever felt like a grasshopper when you looked at all your needs and problems? Does it sometimes seem there are giants lined up against you to keep you from ever receiving something better from life?

Stop seeing poverty and start seeing prosperity

To achieve the success and prosperity God has for you through His Master Plan, you must stop seeing yourself as a slave—defeated, needy, put down and poor. You must start thinking of yourself as successful, prosperous and "on top." Your thinking is critically important, because the Bible says, "As he thinketh in his heart, so is he" (Prov. 23:7).

I heard of one woman who "caught on" to this concept and began to see through the eyes of faith. She even went one step further. On her cupboard and refrigerator doors she taped pictures of all kinds of healthy, nourishing food she wanted to be there instead of the bare essentials and commodity goods she had. She tacked up magazine pictures of just the kind of furniture and accessories she wanted to have on the wall of her living room. In fact, she even had her old, worn out sofa hauled away to make room for the beautiful new one she was expecting God to give her.

This lady had pictures of nice clothes taped to her closets, a picture of a new vacuum cleaner in her broom closet, and two big color pictures of new automobiles on the shelf where she kept her bus tokens.

You may think she was crazy, but I'm told that within a matter of weeks good things started happening to her—exactly the things she was expecting. And within six months every single item she had pictured belonged to her, from a refrigerator full of good food to a new Cadillac!

Now I didn't know this lady personally, but I believe what happened to her. I've seen these kind of miracles take place over and over again. I am personally acquainted with a young Navajo woman named Lorraine Price. She came to one of my crusades on the reservation to share this testimony. She said:

"When I first wrote to you I was having a real struggle with my finances. I had decided to become a partner with God by giving to win souls through God's Master Plan. With my first Master Plan offering I sent in my prayer requests—and it looked like I was asking for a lot. I said I needed a good job, a new vehicle and a new house.

"You wrote back to me saying you had prayed that God would release my finances and I should expect that my needs would all be met by a miracle.

"That is exactly what happened. It would take too long to tell all the details, but God gave me a new job—the best I've ever had, even better than I had hoped for. And I got a new vehicle that is really well-suited to the rough roads here on the reservation. And I'm getting ready to move into my house. God gave me all these things in just a few months, almost before I had time to expect them.

"I'm so glad you showed me how to have something better. I feel that I can serve God better now that I've begun to be blessed in every part of my life."

Isn't that a great testimony? And it can be your story too. But the key action for you to take is to stop seeing your poverty and need and start seeing yourself blessed and prosperous.

There was a song I used to hear when I was just a young man that said

You've got to accentuate the positive,
Eliminate the negative,
Latch on to the affirmative.
Don't mess with Mr. In-between.

Now that may not be a Christian song, but it sure preaches the message of God's Master Plan. I believe if you'll sing that for a while you'll see how you should act when you begin to realize who you really are and what God wants you to be.

You can be the way God sees you

By faith, begin to see yourself as the person God wants you to be. Begin to think the way you'd like to think. Start acting the way you'd like to act. Set out to live the way you'd like to

live. Visualize yourself becoming what God said
you could be.

God doesn't see what you have been as much
as He sees what you are going to be. He's not as
much interested in where you've been as where
you're going. He's not as concerned over what
you've done as what you are going to do. He sees
all your potential—your high points, good qualities and positive attributes. And He wants to
make something beautiful of your life.

Do you know what God sees for you? He sees
you coming out of the dust of defeat. He sees
you coming out of sin, sickness and poverty. He
sees you coming out of depression and mental oppression. He sees you coming out of the wilderness and crossing to the Promised Land. And
you can be just the way He sees you.

"God, You've got a problem"

One of my friends has a refreshing way of
looking at life and the difficulties that come
along from time to time. He says, "I belong to
God. Everything I have belongs to God. So when
something goes wrong, I don't worry about it. I
just say, 'God, You've got a problem!' Then I just
depend on the Lord to work everything out for
good according to His Master Plan. And He always does."

Why not give that a try? Instead of struggling
to solve your own problems and meet your own

needs, just dedicate yourself, your family, your job, your entire life and being to the Lord. Then when trouble comes along and knocks on your door, tell the devil he's got the wrong address. It's God's problem. And no problem is too hard for God. With Him, all things are possible.

You are unique—one of a kind

Out of all the people who have ever lived since the dawn of creation, over all the centuries and in all the countries of the world, there has never been another person like you. No one has ever had your mind, heart, eyes, ears, hands, hair or mouth. No one has ever walked, talked, moved or thought like you. You are rare. And like all things rare, you are valuable. In fact, you are God's greatest miracle—His supreme creation. Never again till the end of time will there ever be anyone else exactly like you.

So you are important to God. He made you in His image. And He made you to succeed. He made you to enjoy the best heaven can afford.

"Your Daddy's rich"

With God as your Father, you need never worry about shortages and lack of resources. For He owns it all—everything. "The world is mine, and the fulness thereof" (Ps. 50:12). God says, "The silver is mine, and the gold is mine" (Hag. 2:8).

So the last thing you should be worrying about is where your supply will come from. Don't you know who you are? You are one of God's children. You can claim what you need from your Father. "Your Daddy's rich"—and He wants you to enjoy all He has provided.

Think about these things:
1. Nothing can enslave you but your own thinking. "As a man thinketh in his heart, so is he."

2. Visualize what you want to become and what you want to receive.

3. Begin to see yourself as God sees you—a creation in His image with unlimited potential for success.

4. You are unique, rare, valuable. And you are God's—so all He has belongs to you.

5. Always remember who you are and what you are entitled to as a son of God.

6

How to let go of loneliness

With all my heart I believe God's Master Plan will bring something better into every part of your life. I have said over and over that God will heal you everywhere you hurt—in soul, mind and body.

In the past two decades I have ministered personally to many thousands of people in crusades and rallies all over the world. I have corresponded with thousands more. Through these contacts, I have come to know about the needs and hurts of people—the things that keep them from having the full blessings of God's Master Plan.

At the top of the list of problems is loneliness. We are part of the lonely crowd. The pressures and challenges of our day have produced a world of lonely people jammed together like sardines in the can called earth. Lynn White, Jr., president of Mills College in Oakland, California, summed it up simply by saying, "The great disease of the 20th Century is loneliness."

Loneliness has many causes and expressions

Loneliness is a worn, thin, white-haired figure in a rocking chair on a crumbling front porch—watching in vain for the postman.

Loneliness is scrambling for a seat on a crowded bus or subway, or sitting alone at a coffee shop counter surrounded by hundreds of rushing, babbling people.

Loneliness is feeling small and unimportant up against the vastness of the universe, among the multitudes of people in the world.

Man has created a society on wheels and wings. We move from neighborhood to neighborhood, from city to city, from state to state, even from country to country. And the freedom we have gained has also produced a sense of impermanence, of rootlessness.

Our lives are crammed so full of running fast and working hard that there is no time for friendliness, fellowship—the neighborliness that once was the foundation stone of our country's life.

If for some reason we are not caught up in the hustle and bustle of modern living, we may feel left out, shut off, isolated, alienated. We desperately try to signal the world to stop and pick us up, but it passes by without slowing down or looking our way. After each unsuccessful attempt to break out of our isolation, we feel the damp fog of loneliness settle on our souls, and secretly cry out, "God—I'm lonely."

Have you ever said to a friend, "I'm so lonely I feel like I could die"?

God can heal loneliness

Perhaps we could cope with this unhappy malady if we could pinpoint the one thing that causes it. But that's impossible because there are so many causes. So we constantly struggle to escape it—like trying to put down a ball of sticky tape. The more we try to get rid of it, the tighter it sticks. And we can't find a way to let go of it.

But there is a way. And you can find it.

The way to let go of loneliness is not popularity. Many of Hollywood's most popular superstars, surrounded by fans, fame and fortune, have finally resorted to suicide to try and end the aching needs of their spirit.

Nor is success in itself a cure for loneliness. Ernest Hemingway, whose works are known around the world, said toward the end of his life that he "lived in a vacuum as lonely as a radio tube when the batteries are dead and the current off."

Power and possessions will not cure loneliness. It was the poet Tennyson who visited Queen Victoria and reported, "Up there in her glory and splendor, she was lonely."

What then, is the answer?

Six suggestions to help you be set free

God, our Heavenly Father, has provided an escape from loneliness. It is part of His Master Plan for your life. Start by reminding yourself of these simple truths.

First, God knows who you are. When it seems no one on earth remembers you, or knows where you are, or even cares—God does. Jesus said God keeps such a close watch on you that "The very hairs of your head are all numbered" (Matt. 10:30).

Second, realize you are never alone. When Moses died and Joshua was left with the awesome responsibility of leading the Israelites into Canaan, perhaps no other human being understood how lonely he felt. But God came to Joshua and said, "As I was with Moses, so I will be with thee: I will not fail thee, nor forsake thee . . . be not afraid, neither be thou dismayed: for the Lord thy God is with thee whithersoever thou goest" (Josh. 1:5, 9).

After His crucifixion and resurrection, and just before His ascension, Jesus promised the disciples His personal presence—"And, lo, I am with you alway even unto the end of the world" (Matt. 28:20).

Those promises hold true for you and me

today. We are not alone. Jesus is with us.

Third, our very living is in the fellowship of God. Wherever we may go and whatever circumstances we may get ourselves into, we can be close to God. The Bible says, "For in him we live, and move, and have our being" (Acts 17:28). However isolated you may think you are, your Heavenly Father is not far away, because, "The eternal God is your refuge and dwelling place, and underneath are the everlasting arms" (Deut. 33:27, TAB).

Fourth, remind yourself that God's presence is everywhere. David wrote, "Whither shall I go from thy spirit? or whither shall I flee from thy presence? If I ascend up into heaven, thou art there: if I make my bed in hell, behold thou art there. If I take the wings of the morning, and dwell in the uttermost parts of the sea; Even there shall thy hand lead me, and thy right hand shall hold me" (Ps. 139:7-10).

Fifth, realize there are other people in the world who are lonely too. Once Elijah thought he was all alone as God's persecuted prophet, but the Lord reminded him He had 7,000 others who were still faithful to Him (1 Kings 19:14-18).

Look around you. Do you see any other people who are struggling with loneliness too? Then reach out to them. It's amazing how we can overcome our own loneliness when we take the initiative and seek out others who are down. As we help them, we help ourselves.

Someone once said, "People are lonely because they build walls instead of bridges." Try building a bridge to help some other lonely person escape from his isolation. And when he crosses over into the freedom of fellowship, you will walk with him, free at last.

Finally, get involved in God's work. Too many Christians suffer from loneliness because they are *sitting* instead of *serving*. If you are isolated, it may be God's way of allowing you to have time to do some of the things you've been neglecting—things like praying and studying the Word of God.

Finding your place of service in the Kingdom of God is a sure way to develop friendship, fellowship and relationships with other Christians. As you become more involved, you'll find that loneliness will strike far less often.

This is part of the benefits of God's Master Plan. It gives you an opportunity to be part of something worthwhile—a soul-winning ministry that is carrying out God's Great Commission in many ways and many places around the world. Your faithful partnership giving makes you a part of all that is accomplished. You are needed. You are important. You belong.

So there you have it—several ways you can let go of loneliness and find fulfillment—something better through God's Master Plan. Perhaps the best way to sum it all up is in the words of this grand old gospel song:

> How can I be lonely, when I've Jesus only
> To be my companion and unfailing guide?
> How can I be weary, or my pathway dreary,
> When He's walking by my side?

Thoughts to remember:
1. All of us are vulnerable to loneliness sometimes.

2. There are ways to let go of loneliness and keep it from destroying your life.

3. Some of the answers are:
   - Realize God knows who you are (Matt. 10:30).
   - Realize you are never alone (Josh. 1:5-9 and Matt. 28:20).
   - Understand that you live, move and exist in the presence and being of God (Acts 17:28).
   - Realize there are other people in the world who are lonely too (1 Kings 19:14-18).
   - Get involved in God's work through His Master Plan (Luke 6:38).

"Teaching
them to observe
all things whatsoever
I have commanded you:
and, lo, I am with you
alway, even unto the end
of the world. Amen."
(MATT. 28:20)

7

Plant what you've got and harvest what you need

"I really like the idea of this God's Master Plan program," a man said to me some time ago. "I sure hope it works for me. I'm going to tell God I am willing to do something for Him sometime if He'll go ahead and bless me now. Then, when I get prosperous and can pay off all my bills and get a little bit ahead, I'll consider starting to pay something to the church, or maybe even to some other religious works."

"I can tell you right now God's Master Plan is not going to work for you," I said to the man.

"Why not?" he asked.

"Because God's Master Plan is not something for nothing. It is a simple, Bible-based program that depends entirely upon you obeying God's formulas for success. You can't go switching things around and still expect those formulas to work. All of God's commands require you to put Him first—'Give, and it shall be given . . . Seek

ye first the Kingdom, then these things shall be
added.' "

Receiving begins with giving

There are no short cuts. If you want to receive
something from God, you must first give something to Him. He will take what you have to
give and, by a miracle, use it to supply what you
need. Jesus' very first miracle during His
earthly ministry was providing wine for a
marriage celebration. But He did not simply
cause empty containers to be full. He first
required that something be given. In this case it
was nothing more than water—which was all
the servants had to give. But when they gave
that, the need was supplied with a fresh, deluxe
supply of the very best wine (see John 2).

Receiving begins with giving. Luke 6:38
says, "Give, and it shall be given unto you." In
fact, that verse goes on to say that "with the
same measure that ye mete withal it shall be
measured to you again."

Does that mean you're just going to get back
the same thing you give? Not at all. The
servants at the wedding in Cana got back wine
for water. God takes what you have and gives
back what you need. But that's not all. Even
when He uses the same measure, He finds a
way to give you more, "good measure, pressed
down, and shaken together, and running over."

You'll get more out if you put more in

Years ago a young boy went with his preacher father far out in the country to minister at a very small church. This particular congregation had a collection box at the door in which members were supposed to put their offerings. When the boy and his father arrived, they both put an offering in the box—a quarter each. Then they went inside for the service.

After church was over, the preacher was told he was entitled to take whatever was in the collection box as his payment for coming. When he opened the box, out fell exactly 50 cents— two quarters.

The little boy watched it all, then looked up at his dad and said, "Well, I guess we'd have got more out if we'd put more in!"

The truth is, the more you give to God, the more He gives to you. To a large extent you control how much God can bless you by how much material you give Him to work with. The Apostle Paul expressed it this way, "He which soweth sparingly shall reap also sparingly; and he which soweth bountifully shall reap also bountifully" (2 Cor. 9:6).

The laws of the harvest

God's Master Plan is based on some definite, clear-cut, unchanging laws God has set in motion in the universe. Observing and obeying these laws make it possible for us to know in advance that certain things will happen in our lives. Let's look at God's three laws of the harvest. The first is very simple.

1. Like begets like. This was God's plan from the beginning. During creation, "God said, Let the earth bring forth grass, the herb yielding seed, and the fruit tree yielding **fruit after his kind,** whose seed is in itself" (Gen. 1:11). That means if you plant corn, you get corn back. If you sow wheat, wheat will come up. If you plant apple seeds, an apple tree will grow. Like produces like. So you don't plant peanuts to get watermelons. That's one of God's laws.

The Bible says, "Be not deceived; God is not mocked: for whatsoever a man soweth, that shall he also reap" (Gal. 6:7).

2. One seed planted multiplies when grown. Jesus said, "Except a corn of wheat fall into the ground and die, it abideth alone: but if it die, it bringeth forth much fruit" (John 12:24).

Wouldn't it be a tremendous hardship if you planted one kernel of corn in the ground and when harvest time finally came months later, you got one kernel of corn back? Or if you had to plant a peach seed and wait several seasons for the tree to grow large enough to finally produce one peach?

But that's not the way God planned it. One seed planted gives back an abundance. I'm told a single kernel of corn will produce between 700 and 800 other kernels. That's the way God will multiply blessings back to you when you give to Him.

3. Seed planted in a cultivated, fertilized, well-watered field will produce a bumper crop. Jesus taught that seed put in good ground would be productive. Seed that falls in unprepared areas will be lost (Hag. 1:6). So if you are careful to put your giving in a ministry that is well managed and dedicated completely to God's work, you are guaranteed results.

The psalmist promised that, "He that goeth forth and weepeth, bearing precious seed, shall doubtless come again with rejoicing, bringing his sheaves with him" (Ps. 126:6). Did you notice the guarantee? He shall *doubtless* come again—without a doubt—for sure! And while he went forth with seeds, he came back with sheaves. "Cast thy bread upon the waters: for thou shalt find it after many days" (Eccles. 11:1).

Where should your giving go?

People often ask me how they can know where they should pay their tithes and give their offerings. Those are questions I cannot answer for everybody. I know we are responsible for the "seed" God entrusts to us. We are not to plant it in just any field and say, "I'm only responsible for planting—what happens to it after that is someone else's worry."

I do know this—the Bible teaches that the tithe is the Lord's—the firstfruit, the 10 percent. It is to be given to Him. And we know He uses what is given by believers to further the Kingdom of God and support His church.

But what is the church? It is the entire body of Christ—people who have been called to follow Jesus and do His will. Buildings and denominational organizations are not the church. The entire congregation of believers in the world is the body of Christ.

Within that church, God has many ministries. The Bible says, "And he gave some, apostles; and some, prophets; and some, evangelists; and some, pastors and teachers; For the perfecting of the saints, for the work of the ministry, for the edifying of the body of Christ" (Eph. 4:11-12).

So if you believe these offices and callings are of God, then they are worthy of your support. If God uses the tithe to care for His church, that must include all His offices—apostles, prophets, evangelists, pastors and teachers. God is teaching us the laws of the harvest. We are responsible to see that the seeds of our tithes and offerings are planted in ministries that are getting something done—that we believe will produce a harvest.

Don't plant posies when you need potatoes

When we understand God's laws of the harvest, we can see that we get what we give. So to receive what we need from God, it is obvious what we must give to Him. We certainly won't get a food crop by planting flower seeds.

If you need a money blessing, plant a money seed. Give out of your need and watch what happens. If you need more time, give God some of the time you do have. Time will come to you, saved from other places. Do you need friends? Give friendship to someone else. Do you need prayer? Find someone else who has the same need and concentrate all your prayer power on them.

The answer is that basic—that simple. Give what you need. Plant seeds of what you must have, and God will give it to you in abundant supply.

Nothing happens until somebody gives something

A few years ago a skilled sales convention speaker named Red Motley coined a phrase that said, "Nothing happens until somebody sells something." Well, in God's Master Plan, nothing happens until somebody gives something to God.

You know the story of the widow who received a miracle supply of oil and meal. Well, nothing happened until she used what seemed to be the last of her supply to prepare a meal for Elijah.

Jesus borrowed one of Peter's boats as a platform to preach to a multitude of people gathered on a lake shore. Afterward, He told Peter to launch out into the deep and let down his nets for a catch. So many fish were caught that it took two boats to hold them and then they started sinking. The nets were breaking—it was the largest catch of fish anyone has ever heard of from that body of water. But before the fish were caught, the use of the boat was given to God (Luke 5:1-7).

Do you remember when the 5,000 were fed from the loaves and fishes? Afterward, the leftover fragments gathered up filled 12 baskets. There was more than enough to meet the need. But before there was plenty left over a little boy had to give Jesus his lunch of bread and fish.

But in each case, nothing happened until somebody gave something to God. If the widow had not made a cake for Elijah—no multiplied oil and meal. (1 Kings 17:10-16). If Peter had not given his boat to the Lord—no miracle catch of fish. If the lad had not given his lunch to Jesus—no 12 baskets of leftover fragments. And if you do not put God first in your giving— no something better blessing to meet your needs.

Seven characteristics of sowing and reaping

Let's take a moment to review some of the things we have learned about God's unchangeable laws of the harvest. There are at least seven key truths that are important secrets for success.

1. Reaping is only possible when there has been something sown.
2. You can reap only what has been sown— like produces like.
3. You always reap in a different season than you sowed in. You must wait for the harvest.
4. You will reap more than you sow.
5. You will reap in proportion to what you sowed.
6. You will reap a full harvest if you remain faithful and keep cultivating, fertilizing and watering the fields you have planted.
7. You cannot change last year's harvest. Forget it and immediately begin on this year's.

Giving is the key to happiness

I've shared a great deal of information with you in this chapter. Do the things I've told you about really work? Here's a letter from a lady in New York who says they do. She writes:

Dear Rev. Stewart,
 I want to share with you what God is

doing for me. I'm so excited I can hardly sit still as I write. The reason is, God is blessing me in all I do. I'm enjoying *all* of God's blessings. You may not get a letter like this often, but God has poured me out a blessing that I can't hold—He does all I ask of Him and more.

I want you to know God's Master Plan sure works for me. I find that *giving is the key to happiness.* I'm so happy I've learned how to give because I find that my blessing and my joy really come through my giving. I love to give now.

Thank you for showing me how to share in doing God's work through God's Master Plan. I've never been so blessed as I am now. I wouldn't miss sending my part to help in your work. I sure know I can't beat God giving.

Mable Davenport, New York

Points in review:

  1. God's Master Plan is not something for nothing. There are no short cuts to God's blessings. Receiving always begins with giving.

  2. There are three basic laws of the harvest— like begets like; one seed planted multiplies when grown; and seed planted in a cultivated, fertilized, well-watered field will produce a bumper crop.

3. You are responsible for your giving. Be sure gifts are being used productively to minister to the church and carry out the Great Commission.

4. Give what you need to receive. That is the first step to having your needs supplied.

8

You lose what you hold onto and multiply what you give away

Perhaps the hardest part of God's Master Plan to understand in the natural is the importance God places on giving—the absolute necessity for being a channel through which blessings flow rather than a container to bottle them up.

The underlying concept of the Lord's prosperity and success plan is that you lose what you hold onto, and multiply what you give away. This is a life principle that applies to everybody, in every part of their existence.

The wisest man who ever lived, the great Solomon, declared, "There is that scattereth, and yet increaseth; and there is that withholdeth more than is meet, but it tendeth to poverty. The liberal soul shall be made fat: and he that watereth shall be watered also himself" (Prov. 11:24-25).

It's really a very simple lesson. If a farmer "gives away" the grain he has by scattering it in the prepared fields, it is increased to him—

multiplied back many times over. But if he tries to hold onto most of what he has and plant only a little, poverty comes his way. Why? Because the harvest will be very small, and the grain he had hoarded up will soon be consumed.

How much better to carry out God's Master Plan by giving. Then, "he who gives seed to the sower and bread for food will supply and multiply your seed and cause the fruits of your righteousness to grow" (2 Cor. 9:10, Lamsa).

Do you believe it? Jesus said, "He that believeth on me, as the scripture hath said, out of his belly shall flow rivers of living water" (John 7:38).

In Luke 19 we can read a parable Jesus told about some servants who were given a certain amount of their master's money to manage while he was gone on a trip. One servant tried to hold on tight to what he was given, and he accomplished nothing. If there was inflation back in those days, I suppose the value of what he had to give back to his master was really less than he was originally given. But the other servants seemed to understand the principle of multiplying by giving away. They put their funds to work and were able to report increases of five to 10 times.

The principle works for seeds, it works for money—it works for every other part of human experience. You lose what you hold onto, and multiply what you give away. It even works with love.

Try keeping all your affection for yourself, sharing none of it with anyone else. Your love will shrivel up and die. But start giving it away, sharing it with others, and love begins to multiply and flow back to you in a mighty stream. In fact, Jesus said love would become the badge of identification for His disciples. "By this shall all men know that ye are my disciples, if ye have love one to another" (John 13:35).

There's nothing worse than wormy manna

There are some things you simply can't save by not using. Time is one of them. Use your time, give it away and you get much accomplished. Try saving it by not using it and you lose it all.

When the children of Israel were out in the wilderness, God fed them with manna, a kind of white wafer that was good only for one day. God commanded that they gather a fresh supply each morning and not try to hoard up a stockpile. Some of the people did not listen. They tried keeping some stale manna—"and it bred worms, and stank" (Exod. 16:20). They lost what they tried to keep.

The curse of stinginess

What happens if we do not give as God commands? What if we try to hoard and hold onto everything that comes our way?

The Bible says we are robbing God, and that we are cursed with a curse (Mal. 3:8-9). If we do not pay our tithes and give our offering to God, then we miss the blessings He promises—multiplied blessings "that there shall not be room enough to receive" (Mal. 3:10). Instead, just the opposite comes upon us.

The first curse of stinginess is that there is no meat in God's house (v. 10). Across America and around the world there are churches that are barely operating. Many of them can hardly afford to pay the interest on the mortgages and loans. Just like individuals, churches that don't give to God go broke.

The second part of the curse is that the windows of heaven are closed. God said if we gave He would open the windows of heaven. So it stands to reason that if we don't give, the windows stay closed. And the churches literally dry up—they get so dusty and dead that no one can live in them. They become museums—mausoleums.

Third, when we are stingy, the devourer is turned loose. He has free rein over those who do not obey God. And he inflicts the curse of destruction upon the disobedient. It sometimes seems that more business schemes of disobedient Christians go aground than for any other group of people in the world. They are victims of the devourer.

Next, we see that by not giving, we are cursed by our vines casting forth half-ripe fruit. I'm not making all this up—just look for yourself at Mal. 3:11! A person living with the curse of stinginess may buy a piece of real estate and hold it for years and somehow it will fail to increase in value. Another person can buy that same property and in a matter of months double his money. Why? Under the curse, our vines cast forth half-ripe fruit.

There's still more. The Bible says those who rob God will not be called blessed by the nations of the earth. And last, instead of being delightsome, the stingy church becomes burdensome upon the land.

God's principle holds true—you lose what you hold onto and multiply what you give away. Whatever you do don't try to save what God wants you to give. Instead, invest it into His work and let Him bless you with a multiplied increase.

Three rules for giving

There are three easy rules to follow when you give that will produce guaranteed results. Patterning your giving after these Bible guidelines will help you receive the something better blessings that God intends you to have through

His Master Plan.

Give willingly. "Let everyone give as his heart tells him, neither grudgingly nor under compulsion, for God loves the man who gives cheerfully. After all, God can give you everything that you need, so that you may always have sufficient for yourselves and for giving away to other people" (2 Cor. 9:7-8, Phillips).

Give generously. "For God, who gives seed to the farmer to plant, and later on, good crops to harvest and eat, will give you more and more seed to plant and will make it grow so that you can give away more and more fruit from your harvest" (2 Cor. 9:10, TLB).

Give confidently. Having obeyed God's command to give, you may expect something better to flow into your life like a mighty river. You can ask what you will and be sure the Lord will answer. But you must give—and ask—confidently. "But let him ask in faith, nothing wavering. For he that wavereth is like a wave of the sea driven with the wind and tossed. For let not that man think that he shall receive any thing of the Lord" (James 1:6-7).

So being confident is important. It is an expression of faith. When you can give willingly, generously and confidently, nothing can keep you from being blessed. God says, "Surely blessing I will bless thee, and multiplying I will multiply thee" (Heb. 6:14).

The key to success is putting God first

A good friend of mine in southern Arizona recently shared a testimony that pretty well sums up all I have been sharing with you in this chapter. His name is Karol George, and he is an extremely successful contractor and builder. He believes the key to success is putting God first.

Because my family was so very poor when I was growing up, I purposed in my heart that by the time I was 30 I would be rich enough that I'd never have to work again in my life.

After I was out of school, I worked hard in the farming and timber business, often putting in 16-hour days. I had set financial goals for myself and I was well on my way to achieving them. I expected to be financially independent while I was still a young man.

But God began dealing with me. I gave my heart to the Lord during a revival at our church, and my life made an abrupt change. God began changing my goals and ambitions. The things I'd worked so long and hard for seemed to lose their value and importance. In fact, I became convinced that God wanted me to get rid of all the things I had placed my confidence in and just trust Him. Instead of holding onto everything, I felt it was time to give them away.

Actually, I had an auction and sold all my property, all my cattle, every piece of equipment and machinery. But some of it sold for so little it was almost like giving it away. I remember watching the sale with tears running down my cheeks.

After the auction my wife and I moved to Arizona with all we had in the world—a car, our clothes and a few personal belongings. I began working, building houses. At about the same time I was introduced to the Bible principles of giving to God and expecting Him to provide for our needs.

We believed this teaching and incorporated it into our lives. And sure enough, I was blessed financially by every job I did. But more important, I was blessed in my spirit as I saw God's Master Plan prove itself over and over.

Our business started with a few houses, but it's grown far beyond our expectations. We wanted to be a reputable company and do a good job for the people we work for. And we have had more success than we could have imagined when we set our goals.

Our business has grown so fast that recently a whole year's goals were reached within a few months. We have 60 or 70 homes under construction at all times in addition to the commercial work we do. We're building close to 200 homes a year in southern Arizona.

I believe the key to success is putting God first. I'm still a fairly young man, but being rich doesn't matter to me any more. I'm rich in the things of God. I can sit at my desk and say, "God, You're first. You are my Partner in business and life. You come first in every area of my life."

Thoughts to remember:

1. You lose what you hold onto, but multiply what you give away. That is a foundation principle of God's laws of prosperity.

2. A stingy attitude toward God brings a curse of suffering and poverty that can destroy you.

3. Giving willingly, generously and confidently is a guaranteed formula for success. It will bring God's blessing to you without fail.

4. The key to success is putting God first.

"There is that
scattereth, and yet
increaseth."
(PROV. 11:24)

9

What is that in your hand?

You already possess the seeds for your success.

The keys to your prosperity are well within your reach.

Like the poor man who unknowingly built his tar paper shack in the middle of acres of diamonds, you are surrounded on every side with unlimited resources.

You don't have to wait until the economy takes a turn for the better. You don't have to wait for your "ship to come in." And you don't have to wait for some rich uncle to leave you a fortune.

The secret you've been looking for in this book is right here—*What do you have in your hand?* Are you willing to give it to God?

If you can answer these questions properly, you can become a force for good that will change your life, your family, your community—perhaps even your nation and the world. God wants to know what you've got, and if you're willing to use it in His Kingdom.

The rod of Moses

When God spoke to Moses from the burning bush, the first question He asked him was, "What is that in thine hand?" (Exod. 4:2).

Moses answered, "A rod."

The rod was very important to Moses. As a shepherd out in the desert, the rod was his staff to direct and herd the sheep. It was his protection against any wild creature or enemy that might come against him or his animals. It was his support to lean on when he was weary from the sun and the long miles of wandering.

God said, "Throw it down."

How Moses must have hated to give up his only security. But he obeyed the Lord. When he threw down the rod, it became a serpent, and Moses started running from it. I don't know how you feel about snakes, but I probably would have done the same thing.

But God wasn't through. He told Moses to go pick up the snake by the tail. I don't know a lot about snakes, but I'm pretty sure you're supposed to pick them up—not by the tail—but behind the head so they won't be able to bite you. But when Moses touched that serpent's tail, it became a rod again.

Sometimes the things God leads us to do don't seem to make a lot of sense by human reasoning.

But the Lord has a plan for us greater than we could ever dream of. "O the depth of the riches both of the wisdom and knowledge of God! How unsearchable are his judgments, and his ways past finding out" (Rom. 11:33). "For my thoughts are not your thoughts, neither are your ways my ways, saith the Lord" (Isa. 55:8).

The rod of God

Someone has pointed out three key verses in the fourth chapter of Exodus. Verse 2 is where God asks, "What is that in thine hand?" Verse 17 shows us that something very strange has happened. God speaks again to Moses and says, "And thou shalt take *this rod* in thine hand." Do you see the difference in tone? Verse 2 is definitely referring to Moses' rod—the one he has in his hand.

But in verse 17, it is almost as if God was standing before Moses, holding out a rod and saying, "Here, take this in your hand." It is as if God had taken the rod and was now offering it back.

The next key scripture is verse 20. It says simply, "And Moses took the *rod of God* in his hand." Do you see what has happened? Moses' rod has been changed to the rod of God. By taking that divine instrument, Moses set out to change the world. He was about to shake the nation of Egypt to its very foundations, and deliver captive Israel from 400 years of bondage.

With his staff, Moses had been a shepherd. But with the rod of God, He became a conqueror.

With his staff, Moses had wandered on the back side of the desert talking to sheep. With the rod of God, he stood boldly in Pharaoh's palace.

With his staff, Moses had been isolated and all alone. With the rod of God, he became the leader of a great nation.

The rod of God made the difference. It was that rod that did signs and wonders in Pharaoh's palace. It was that rod that parted the Red Sea. It was that rod that smote the rock and brought forth water.

Moses' rod was limited to what he could do with it. But the rod of God had unlimited power—it was connected to the full forces of heaven.

But absolutely nothing would have happened if Moses had not thrown down his rod. He had to give it up. And that's exactly what you must do. What do you have in your hand? What is your most prized possession? Is it your job, your business, your livelihood? Is it your house, car, furniture, music, family—or some talent or ability? What is the one thing you count on and depend on the most?

Are you willing to give it to the Lord?

"Oh," you say, "ask me for anything but that.

Don't make me give that up. Why does God want me to throw that down?"

Because He wants you to trust Him completely. And when you do, He will give you back something far greater than you could ever sacrifice for Him. But first you must be willing to make the sacrifice.

Until there is sacrifice, there is no giving

Lots of people are willing to give things they don't care about. But God doesn't want things— He wants you. And when you give the thing closest to your heart, He knows you are giving yourself to Him. That's when He can do something for you.

Too often we are like the people who used to pack missionary barrels to go overseas. They would fill them up with cast-offs—worn out clothes, shoes that didn't fit anymore, mismatched dishes and just plain junk. But God doesn't want your junk—He wants your best.

The Bible tells how David wanted to build an altar and offer a sacrifice to God one day. A man said to him, "Here, take what you need. Here are some oxen you can kill, and some wooden implements you can burn." But King David refused to accept the items as a gift. He paid the man 50 shekels of silver for them, saying, "neither will I offer burnt offerings unto the Lord my God of that which doth cost me nothing" (2 Sam. 24:24).

Maybe you should take a look at what you've been giving to God. Have you just been giving what you felt you could afford, or have you been sacrificing to put God first in your giving? Have you been sharing only gifts that cost you nothing? Then maybe you haven't really been giving at all.

"For unto whomsoever much is given, of him shall be much required: and to whom men have committed much, of him they will ask the more" (Luke 12:48). The reason for this is that God doesn't look at how much you give as much as He does at what you have left. He once said a poor widow who gave only two mites had given more than rich men who put large sums into the treasury at the Temple. Why? "For all they did cast in of their abundance; but she of her want did cast in all that she had, even all her living" (Mark 12:44).

How to succeed when you've already failed

One man said, "There's no use in you talking to me about being successful because I'm already a failure. I've lost all I had and wasted all my opportunities. It's too late for me."

I reminded that man he was in exactly the same shape as the prodigal son when he came to himself in the far country. He had left his father's house, wasted all his inheritance in riotous living, lost all his friends, and was feeding pigs—even wishing he could eat with them.

But when he went back to the father, he was blessed beyond his hopes and expectations. He became part of his father's success, with all the rights and privileges of the father. He was greeted with a kiss, given a robe, a ring, and new shoes—plus he feasted on the fatted calf at a party with all his friends.

Not bad for a failure, would you say? I've always liked this story of how God can take us at our worst and make us examples of righteousness, prosperity and fellowship.

Sometimes I wonder if God doesn't have to let us fail on our own so He can show us how He can make us successful through His Master Plan. At any rate, just because you haven't been successful in the past even trying as hard as you could doesn't mean you can't be successful now.

When you get right down to it, Moses was a failure. You see, he had started out in Pharaoh's palace. When his mother hid him in the bulrushes and he was found by Pharaoh's daughter, he was adopted into the royal family. But he managed to mess up his opportunity. He killed an Egyptian, and was forced to flee like a criminal. In fact, that's how he ended up out on the back side of the desert tending sheep.

He was still there 40 years later when God spoke to him through the burning bush. That's when God traded rods with him and made Moses successful.

So the fact you have failed is no reason to believe you can't be successful now. God is ready to bless you now if you're ready to receive it.

Be part of the answer instead of part of the problem

Once you discover that what you have been doing doesn't work, be ready to try God's way. Resolve that you will not become part of the problem. By obeying the principles of God's Master Plan, you can become part of the answer.

You have all it takes to receive a miracle from God—a miracle of abundant supply. You have a need. Your need is the material God will use to produce a miracle in your life.

But you must give God a free hand to work out the solution to your problems. You must give Him what you have, just as Moses gave his rod.

When you do that, God will give you something better. That's how God's Master Plan works.

What happens when you put God first?

Take a look at these terrific testimonies of what happens when you put God first. They express this truth even better than I can tell you.

What is that in your hand?

Dear Rev. Stewart,

It took all the money I had to send in my God's Master Plan payment. I didn't know where I was going to get money to buy food to eat. That very night an uncle from New York came to visit and gave me $40 and my daughter $25. I am still thanking God for teaching me about God's Master Plan. It really works.

Mrs. Fannie Geddie, North Carolina

From Washington State comes this letter from Mr. and Mrs. Frank Lee.

Dear Rev. Stewart,

Right after we started sending our God's Master Plan payment each month, the Lord sent us a large sum of money. My husband got his paycheck on Friday for over $500. Then on Monday, they gave him another check for $500. He tried to give it back, thinking it was a mistake. But they said, "No, that is your money!" To this day we don't know where it came from . . . except that it was a something better blessing from God. We know for sure that God's Master Plan works.

Never forget:
1. The answer to your problems and needs is

117

already in your hands. God will take what you give Him and use it to give you a miracle provision.

2. Be sure your gift is valuable to you. Until there is sacrifice, there is no giving.

3. Realize that when you have failed, you're just ready for God to help you succeed.

4. Be ready to become part of the answer instead of part of the problem as God guides your actions.

5. Put God first in your life by giving out of your need. That's the way to receive God's best for you.

"For my thoughts
are not your thoughts,
neither are your ways my
ways, saith the Lord."
(ISA. 55:8)

10

The Kingdom keys to prosperity

God's Master Plan always works when you follow its simple principles with sincere faith in God. It has to work because it is based 100% on the Bible, God's Holy Word. And we know His Word cannot fail.

Time and time again I have outlined three basic steps for getting started with God's Master Plan. Let me repeat them once again for you.

First, trust God as your Supplier. Don't put your trust in man, jobs, banks, governments or any other source. Realize that God is your source of supply. "But my God shall supply all your need according to his riches in glory by Christ Jesus" (Phil. 4:19).

Second, put God first by giving. The Lord will not take second place in your life to anybody or anything. He must be the most important thing in your life, and you must put Him first. The best way to do this and express the way you feel toward Him is by giving. "Give, and it shall be given unto you" (Luke 6:38).

Third, expect something better. Whatever you do, don't leave out this essential step to receiving from God. So many people do the first two things and quit. Then they wonder why God's Master Plan doesn't work for them as fully as it does for others. You must expect something better. This is the final demonstration of your faith in action.

When you flip the switch, you expect the light to come on. When a farmer puts seeds in the ground, he expects a harvest. When a fisherman puts his nets or hooks in the water, he expects to catch a fish. If you flipped the switch and never opened your eyes, or if the farmer never went back to his field, or the fisherman never checked to see what was caught—the miracle they started would never be realized.

Expecting is a vital step in the process of receiving something better. "What things soever ye desire, when ye pray, believe that ye receive them, and ye shall have them" (Mark 11:24).

You can't beat God giving

Why does giving through God's Master Plan produce such great results? The primary reason is that it fulfills the Bible conditions for God's prosperity blessings. Then, every dollar you send is used to help to do God's work—to carry out soulwinning outreaches like crusades, missions, literature publication and distribution, Bible schools, television and other ministries. When you give to God, He takes what you invest and uses it to meet your needs as well. You just can't beat God giving, no matter how hard you try.

Nine prosperity principles you can read in your Bible

The Bible is full of suggestions and rules for obtaining blessings from God. I've already shared many of them with you. In this chapter I want to list nine more. I suggest you read and study these until they are as familiar to you as your own name. Then keep this list in a convenient place for frequent reference. When you feel things aren't going as well as they should, read over these Kingdom keys to prosperity and use them to unlock the doors to God's something better in every part of your life.

1. Keep God's Word

If you want to claim the promises of the Bible, you must obey the commandments of the Bible. "Keep therefore the words of this covenant, and do them, that ye may prosper in all that ye do" (Deut. 29:9).

2. Believe God's man

Find a man of God who is preaching and

living God's Word. Believe what he teaches—
obey his instructions. "Believe in the Lord your
God, so shall ye be established; believe his
prophets, so shall ye prosper" (2 Chron. 20:20).
You will be rewarded for receiving and obeying
the man of God. "He that receiveth a prophet in
the name of a prophet shall receive a prophet's
reward" (Matt. 10:41).

3. Seek the Lord

According to the dictionary, *seek* means to
take pains to find. So if you want to enjoy God's
prosperity in your life, take pains to find the
Lord. My Bible says, "As long as he sought the
Lord, God made him to prosper" (2 Chron.
26:5).

4. Live a righteous life

"Blessed is the man that walketh not in the
counsel of the ungodly, nor standeth in the way
of sinners, nor sitteth in the seat of the scornful.
But his delight is in the law of the Lord; and in
his law doth he meditate day and night. And he
shall be like a tree planted by the rivers of
water, that bringeth forth his fruit in his
season; his leaf also shall not wither; and
whatsoever he doeth shall prosper" (Ps. 1:1-3).

5. Be a tither

"Bring ye all the tithes into the storehouse,

that there may be meat in mine house, and prove me now herewith, saith the Lord of hosts, if I will not open you the windows of heaven, and pour you out a blessing that there shall not be room enough to receive it" (Mal. 3:10).

6. Put God first
"Therefore take no thought, saying, What shall we eat? or, Wherewithal shall we be clothed? for your heavenly Father knoweth that ye have need of all these things. But seek ye first the kingdom of God, and his righteousness; and all these things shall be added unto you" (Matt. 6:31-33).

7. Always give before you receive
"Give, and it shall be given unto you; good measure, pressed down, and shaken together, and running over, shall men give into your bosom. For with the same measure that ye mete withal it shall be measured to you again" (Luke 6:38).

8. Give willingly and generously
"But this I say, He which soweth sparingly shall reap also sparingly; and he which soweth bountifully shall reap also bountifully. Every man according as he purposeth in his heart, so let him give; not grudgingly, or of necessity: for God loveth a cheerful giver. And God is able to

make all grace abound toward you; that ye, always having all sufficiency in all things, may abound to every good work" (2 Cor. 9:6-8).

9. Believe the promises and patiently wait for their fulfillment

God sets His own timetable. No one can say exactly when God will answer prayer, or send the blessings of prosperity cascading into your life. The important thing is—He will! "And let us not be weary in well doing: for in due season we shall reap, if we faint not" (Gal. 6:9). "And so, after he had patiently endured, he obtained the promise" (Heb. 6:15).

And now, read these testimonies from people who have proved His promises are true.

For the first time in my life I know where I'm going and what I want to do

I've been so happy since I joined God's Master Plan. God has really blessed me and I know now what it means to put Him first. My money seems to go so much farther. All my bills are paid up-to-date and I haven't been able to do that for a long time. After I pay my faith promise to God I still have money left over. For the first time in my life I know where I'm going and what I want to do.

Ruby Alexander, Illinois

We thought there was no way out of our financial problems

We are being blessed when we put God first in our lives. About a month ago when we started God's Master Plan, my wife got a job at the airport and also a part-time job working in a local hotel. This is really a miracle for us. We thought there was no way out of our financial problems. But I know the Lord's hand is helping ease our problems. Paying our bills no longer seems like a burden to us. They just don't seem as bad as they did before we started using God's Master Plan. We also are receiving spiritual blessings when we put God first.

G. Johnson, Canada

I'd never received a big, unexpected blessing until I started working with God's Master Plan

Good things start to happen when you work with God's Master Plan. I'd never received anything big and unexpected before, but last Saturday a grocery store where I shop gave me $100 worth of groceries absolutely free. I was shocked . . . but so glad for it.

I believe this is just the beginning, and

more good things are in store for me. I'm
not about to stop working with God's Master
Plan.

Lucy Greene, North Carolina

Remember:
1. The three primary keys to God's Master
   Plan are trust, give and expect.

2. It takes all three keys to unlock the fullness
   of what God has for you—something better
   in every part of your life.

3. There are nine prosperity principles that
   will transform your life and change your
   world: Keep God's Word, believe God's
   man, seek the Lord, live righteously, be a
   tither, put God first, always give before
   receiving, give willingly and generously,
   and believe the promises and wait patiently
   for their fulfillment.

Remember, your
Bible keys to success are:
1. Trust—Phil. 4:19
2. Give—Luke 6:38
3. Expect—Mark 11:24

11

Sharing my secrets for success

I was having lunch with a business friend one day. We had been talking about the services his company had been performing for the Don Stewart Evangelistic Association at our Phoenix headquarters office, and what our needs might be in the future. Although he hadn't mentioned it, I knew my friend's business had been having some difficulties.

During our conversation, somehow the subject of God's Master Plan came up. I had given this friend a copy of my book, *How You Can Have SOMETHING BETTER through God's Master Plan*, and he had several copies of our monthly publication, *MIRACLE* magazine.

"You know, Don," he said to me, "this God's Master Plan concept you talk about would probably work pretty good for a guy if everything was going O.K. But how does it work when you're already in trouble? Anybody can be successful when everything works right, but what about when the problems come?"

"That's when God's Master Plan works best," I said. "In fact, the more problems you've got, the better God's Master Plan will work for you."

"Why is that?" he asked.

"Jesus said, 'They that are whole need not a physician; but they that are sick' (Luke 5:31). He was saying, 'Miracles are for people with needs.' "

My friend started smiling. "I get it," he said. "That's why you say—If you have a need, you can have a miracle."

"You're exactly right," I said. Then I began to show him how he could use the principles of God's Master Plan to make his business more successful. When he left the restaurant to go back to work he was so excited he could hardly wait to see what God was going to do for him.

For the past several months I've been noticing in my mail that certain situations and problems seem to be causing trouble for a lot of people. So I've been saving some of the questions people have written to me about to deal with in this book. You may have had one or more of these problems in your life already. If not, one may happen to you soon. I believe God has given me some insight and suggestions to share with you that might help you deal with these detours along the road to success and prosperity.

When you feel like you can't go on

Stop and rest! Most of the time when you feel like this, it's because you are completely exhausted, spiritually, mentally, emotionally, and physically. And the answer is to let God restore you. Stop struggling. Back off and get a fresh look at your situation. "Be still, and know that I am God" (Ps. 46:10).

That's not all. David said, "Commune with your own heart upon your bed, and be still. Offer the sacrifices of righteousness, and put your trust in the Lord" (Ps. 4:4-5).

Isn't that tremendous? The psalmist says you must get back in touch with yourself, rest, spread out the rightness of your efforts before God, and trust in Him.

What will happen then? "They that wait upon the Lord shall renew their strength; they shall mount up with wings as eagles; they shall run, and not be weary; and they shall walk, and not faint" (Isa. 40:31). That means, with God, you will be going on when you thought you couldn't.

When you can't find true happiness

A wise man once said, "Happiness is a state of mind." And it is true that sometimes we are not happy when there seems to be no cause or reason for unhappiness. We can make ourselves miserable by the power of our thinking.

That's why Paul advised, "Let this mind be in

you, which was also in Christ Jesus: Who, being in the form of God, thought it not robbery to be equal with God" (Phil. 2:5-6). Do you think Jesus was happy? Then you can be too.

The Bible is filled with helpful suggestions on how to find true happiness. Jesus listed several in His Sermon on the Mount, which you will find in Matthew 5. If you read verses 3 through 10 in The Living Bible, you will find that happiness comes from your endeavors to be just, good, kind, merciful, pure and peaceable.

Solomon's Proverbs advise that "he that keepeth the law, happy is he," and "Happy is the man that findeth wisdom, and the man that getteth understanding" (Prov. 29:18; 3:13).

God wants you to be happy. It is part of His plan for your life. So instead of seeking for happiness in human relationships, possessions, activities or any other source, look to God. Expect your happiness to come from Him. "Blessings on all who reverence and trust the Lord— on all who obey him! Their reward shall be prosperity and happiness" (Ps. 128:1-2, TLB).

When you need encouragement from someone who doesn't give up

I wrote this book to encourage you. As I said in my introductory chapter, my main purpose in publishing this volume was to help you and others who still needed more assistance in applying the principles of God's Master Plan. It was as if the Lord spoke to me, as He did to Moses, saying, "But charge Joshua, and encourage him, and strengthen him" (Deut. 3:28).

I have not given up on you—and with God's help I never will. I invite you to write to me any time you have a problem to share, or if there is any way at all I can be of help to you.

But let me urge you also to find fellowship in a church of real believers—people who trust God's Word and know how to pray. These kind of people will help and lift you up. This is why God intended us to be part of His church, so there would be many people to encourage us instead of just one or two. This is part of God's Master Plan. "They helped every one his neighbour; and every one said to his brother, Be of good courage" (Isa. 41:6).

I realize sometimes it is not possible to find encouragement at church and sometimes even trusted friends betray you, or grow tired of standing by you. But "there is a friend that sticketh closer than a brother" (Prov. 18:24).

Once David led an army out to fight. When he and his men came back, the enemy had raided their home city, carrying away all their wives and children, and burning their homes. The Bible says David and his men wept, "until they had no more power to weep" (1 Sam. 30:4).

Besides his own personal loss, David felt keenly the losses of his people. Then, they turned against him and talked about stoning him. Do you know what David did in this sad, discouraging time? Here's the answer—"but David encouraged himself in the Lord his God" (1 Sam. 30:6).

And that's what you must do—learn to encourage yourself in the Lord. When all friends forsake you or you are away from all other sources of encouragement—the Lord will always be there.

He never gets tired of ministering to you, either. Once Peter asked Jesus how many times he should forgive a brother who sinned against him—"till seven times?"

Jesus replied, "Until seventy times seven" (Matt. 18:22). If He will forgive that many times, how many more times will He encourage you? Be encouraged today!

When you're tired of figuring out what you're doing wrong

This may sound frivolous—but don't try. Someone is sure to do it for you and announce it in a loud voice.

I'm serious. It's much more worthwhile to concentrate your thinking and energy on what you are doing right than what you are doing wrong. Someone has said that the best way to break a bad habit is to replace it with a good one. Daniel advised King Nebuchadnezzar to "break off thy sins by righteousness" (Dan. 4:27).

Stop trying to figure out all your past failures and sins and how you messed up. Let God forgive you of every shortcoming—*and start fresh.* "Let the wicked forsake his way, and the unrighteous man his thoughts: and let him return unto the Lord, and he will have mercy upon him; and to our God, for he will abundantly pardon" (Isa. 55:7).

Then, concentrate on doing good rather than not doing bad. You'll get much better results. The Bible says, "Let him eschew [avoid, shun] evil, and do good" (1 Pet. 3:11).

When the devil tells you you're a fool

Consider the source of the criticism. The Bible says Satan is the "accuser of our brethren" (Rev. 12:10). John, the beloved disciple, declares, "There is no truth in him . . . for he is a liar, and the father of it" (John 8:44). So do as Jesus did when Satan tempted Him in the wilderness. He said, "Get thee hence, Satan" (Matt. 4:10). And the devil had to go. Don't listen to the devil. "Resist the devil, and he will flee from you" (James 4:7).

When you pray and nothing happens and your faith takes a beating

I know and believe that God hears and answers our prayers—all of them. Oh, I don't mean He always gives us everything we want. Sometimes God does say, "No." But when that happens, His Spirit deals with us and we know God is responding to our prayer.

Sometimes, though, we pray and it feels as if the heavens are brass—that our prayer didn't go anywhere. Absolutely nothing seems to happen.

There is a Bible explanation for this. Paul says, "For we wrestle not against flesh and blood, but against principalities, against powers, against the rulers of the darkness of this world, against spiritual wickedness in high places" (Eph. 6:12). That means the devil is actively trying to keep your prayers from being answered. He is fighting, battling, warring against you.

Once Daniel prayed and fasted for three weeks before the answer came. Then it was personally delivered by an angel. He told Daniel, "Your request has been heard in heaven and was answered the very first day you began to fast before the Lord and pray . . . that very day I was sent here to meet you. But for twenty-one days the mighty Evil Spirit who overrules the kingdom of Persia blocked my way. Then Michael, one of the top officers of the heavenly army, came to help me, so that I was able to break through" (Dan. 10:12-13, TLB).

So when you pray and the answer doesn't come right away, don't give up. Keep believing. Stay tuned to God's voice. Trust in the Word of God. "And this is the confidence that we have in him, that, if we ask any thing according to his will, he heareth us: And if we know that he hear us, whatsoever we ask, we know that we have the petitions that we desired of him" (1 John 5:14-15).

When the thing that means the most to you slips away just when you thought you had it

So you're disappointed. Well, it's not the end of the world, no matter how bad you feel right now. Disappointment is part of life, and it's important to know how to cope with it. Constant failure to reach your goals or see your plans fulfilled can cause you to lose confidence and hope. Then you may want to just give up in despair.

"What's the use? Nothing ever works out for me. Everything always goes wrong. I'm tired of getting my hopes up only to be let down." Ever feel that way—like crawling off in a corner to watch the world go by without even trying to be a part of it?

When I was a child I remember my mother going to the pantry to get a can of string beans on the top shelf. I watched as she stood on her toes to try and get the can. She made a leap for it but instead of getting hold of it the can slipped back further on the shelf and now she couldn't even touch it—it slipped away from her. Then she got a chair and stood on it and reached across the shelf and got the can. God wants to put a chair under you.

Here are three suggestions that may help you keep disappointment from getting you down.

1. Realize God is in control of all circumstances. And He has a definite plan for your life—His Master Plan—for something better. That means your disappointments are God's appointments. Paul's missionary trips were cut short by imprisonment. Then God used that time to reveal Himself to Paul in a greater way, and the "Prison Epistles" of Ephesians, Philippians and Colossians were written. They have blessed multiplied millions—infinitely more than Paul could have ever preached to in person.

So when your plans fall through, or something you wanted badly doesn't work out, realize that all things work together for good (Rom. 8:28). God wants to give you something better—start looking for it to come.

2. When people are involved in your disappointment, as they often are, just remember that people aren't perfect. They're just people, with all kinds of faults and shortcomings. Think how many times you may have been a disappointment to someone else, whether you

meant to be or not. This may make it easier for you to forgive people for doing things that wreck your plans.

3. Remember your goal in life. It should be to "walk, even as he walked" (1 John 2:6). Keeping your eyes on this goal will keep you from being paralyzed by the frustration of disappointment.

When the dark clouds of disappointment fill your sky, apply these simple principles and see how God will clear away the darkness by the light of His presence.

When you think you'll never get well

God wants to heal you everywhere you hurt. His Master Plan is to give you something better in every part of your being. If you have a need, you can have a miracle. But you must want to be healed.

Jesus once ministered to a man who had been sick for 38 years. The first thing He asked the man was, "Wilt thou be made whole?" (John 5:6). Then He raised the man up.

Check yourself to be sure you are not contributing to your illness through bad habits, wrong diet, or not enough exercise and rest. When a person says he wants to be healed, yet knowingly abuses his body, it's hard to believe he is sincere. Even if he does get healed, his sins against God's laws of nature may well bring sickness to him again.

If you want to be healed, God will make you whole. He wants to heal your spirit so you can control your emotions. He wants to heal your body so it throws off disease. He wants to heal your soul so you can conquer sin and wrong attitudes and be free in mind and spirit. He stands before you now, declaring, "I am the Lord that healeth thee" (Exod. 15:26).

What about death? The Bible says quite clearly that "it is appointed unto men once to die" (Heb. 9:27). And, "Precious in the sight of the Lord is the death of his saints" (Ps. 116:15).

Even if it should be the end of days for an individual, God's Word still does not indicate that it is His plan for that person to die in agony and disease, but rather that His servant should depart in peace (Luke 2:29). *You do not have to get deathly sick to die.* I believe a person can live his life in health and happiness until it is time to go to be with Jesus. Then he can lie down to sleep and wake up in heaven.

More than likely, though, God wants you to get well and overcome the sickness that troubles you. Let God speak to you right now. Perhaps you will hear His voice saying, "This sickness is not unto death, but for the glory of God, that the Son of God might be glorified thereby" (John 11:4).

When you lose instead of winning

Losing one battle, or two, doesn't mean you've

lost the war. "Weeping may endure for a night, but joy cometh in the morning" (Ps. 30:5).

God will not fail, and as His child, neither will you. "For whatsoever is born of God overcometh the world: and this is the victory that overcometh the world, even our faith" (1 John 5:4).

André Crouch, the great singer/songwriter, has inspired millions of people with the victorious message of his song, "Through It All."

I thank God for the mountains, and I thank Him for the valleys,
And I thank Him for the storms He's brought me through,
For if I never had a problem, I wouldn't know that God could solve them,
And I'd never know what faith in God could do.

Here's something you must never forget—*the battle is the Lord's.* He will fight for you and through you. "Because greater is he that is in you, than he that is in the world" (1 John 4:4).

And God will win. If you've been losing instead of winning, start letting God win through you. Just say, "Thine, O Lord, is the greatness, and the power, and the glory, and the victory" (1 Chron. 29:11).

Remember:
1. God's Master Plan always works because it is based 100% on the Word of God.
2. When things aren't going right, that's the best time to apply the principles of God's Master Plan. Miracles are for people with needs.
3. Read this chapter often—especially when you are troubled by one of the problems it deals with. I believe these "Secrets For Success" will help you.

12

Send now *prosperity*

Larry and Joy MacKay are long time friends of mine. They're the kind of people who enjoy life. They smile a lot. They have the kind of prosperity that comes from a life attitude of giving, sharing and caring about other people. It's the true prosperity of a giving spirit.

I met them several years ago when they came from their homes in Canada to attend Bible school at Miracle Valley. They were engaged then, but decided to wait until after they finished school to get married. Neither of them had much money, and both found it a real faith challenge just to get by. Their lives were a day-to-day financial struggle.

They got married on graduation day. They were happy, but no richer. Their first assignment was with a small rural church in Illinois for on-the-job ministerial training. From there they moved on to other responsibilities, always seeking to be of service in the Kingdom of God.

They were still struggling financially, but God somehow always met their needs. Their dreams of having a house, furniture, a car—some of the good things—seemed far in the future.

Then the MacKays heard me teach the Bible principles of complete prosperity for body, mind and spirit. As Larry and Joy listened, God spoke to them that He had a place to use their talents that He would take what they had to provide what they needed. They began to understand that God's law of seed and harvest was a pattern for using little to create plenty. But the planting—the action the miracle of abundance depends on—was theirs.

Larry said, "God used the principle of His Master Plan to open my eyes to how I could have His best. I finally realized that I could bring glory to God by having abundance. And once I understood that, I was ready to do something about it right away."

An act of obedience opens the door

That very night, quietly and with tears steaming down their faces, Larry and Joy MacKay put their paycheck in the offering. That $112 seemed like a million dollars to them. It wasn't just an offering—it was an act of obedience.

And it was like opening a door into a new world for them. From that night, God's something better blessings started flowing their way. God began to bless the work of their hands. Step by step He led them into situations where He could use their talents and skills to bless others and be blessed in return.

Larry now holds a responsible position as a purchasing agent and business consultant to a religious organization. He's using his Bible knowledge, his business capabilities and his natural energy creatively and effectively. He is confident his ministry among his business associates is God's Master Plan for him.

The MacKays continue to be committed partners of this ministry through God's Master Plan. They continue to plant seed by giving, expecting God to give a plentiful harvest.

And God is blessing them. One by one, their dreams are becoming realities. God has given them two beautiful children, Kimberly and Michael. They now drive a late model car. And recently they moved into a custom built, four bedroom home with a deluxe swimming pool and a beautiful landscaped yard.

The MacKays believe with all their hearts that it pleases God for their family to live well. The very fact they have more than the bare necessities of life is one way their lives bring glory to Him.

If God's Master Plan will work for these partners, it will work for you. I've seen with my own eyes how God has blessed this couple from penniless Bible school students to a successful, prosperous family. I believe with all my heart God will bless you the same way He's blessing them.

Vow and pay

Real prosperity came to Larry and Joy when they learned to give to God. They vowed to put God first in their lives and they paid that vow. That's exactly what you must do—make a faith promise to put God first by giving to Him.

The Bible says, "Offer unto God thanksgiving; and pay thy vows unto the most High: And call upon me in the day of trouble: I will deliver thee, and thou shalt glorify me" (Ps. 50:14-15).

That reminds me of what happened to the prophet Jonah. You know the story of how he ran from God and was thrown overboard by his shipmates during a terrible storm at sea. God had prepared a great fish to swallow him up. After three days and nights in the belly of the fish, Jonah thought he was about to die. He wrote, "When my soul fainted within me I remembered the Lord: and my prayer came . . . I will sacrifice unto thee with the voice of thanksgiving; I will pay *that* that I have vowed" (Jon. 2:7, 9).

As soon as Jonah resolved to do what he had promised God, the Lord caused the fish to vomit him up on the dry land. God will always give you an opportunity to keep your promise to Him and pay your vows.

What happens when you "Vow, and pay unto the Lord your God" (Ps. 76:11)? "Thou shalt make thy prayer unto him, and he shall hear thee, and thou shalt pay thy vows . . . Then shalt thou lay up gold as dust, and the gold of Ophir as the stones of the brooks. Yea, the Almighty shall be thy defence, and thou shalt have plenty of silver" (Job 22:27, 24-25).

"All things are *now* ready"

Are you ready to receive God's prosperity? Are you ready to have something better through God's Master Plan? Are you tired of the pressure of unpaid bills, creditors and debt? Are you ready to leave the land of poverty, with its fear, worry and anxiety?

If you are saying YES—then here are some instructions for you from my Bible: "Remember ye not the former things, neither consider the things of old. Behold, I will do a new thing; *now* it shall spring forth" (Isa. 43:18-19). Forget the limitations of the past—forget the poverty of the past—God is ready to bless you *now*.

Paul said, *"Now* faith is the substance of things hoped for, the evidence of things not seen" (Heb. 11:1). And David wrote, "Before I was afflicted I went astray: but now have I kept thy word" (Ps. 119:67).

Are you beginning to get the message? *Now* is the time for you to apply God's Master Plan to your life. You've put it off too long already. You must act *now*.

Jesus told a story about a man who gave a great supper and invited the people of the community to come. When all the preparations were completed, he sent his servants to bring them to the feast, saying, "Come; for all things are *now* ready" (Luke 14:17).

But the people he had invited all had excuses why they couldn't come. Some said they had business to attend to, others sent word that personal matters kept them from attending. But the man knew they were all just making excuses. Jesus said the man told his servants to go and bring in the poor, sick and needy to the feast. "Go out into the highways and hedges, and compel them to come in," he said. And those that had been invited first missed out completely.

There is no tomorrow in God's Master Plan

God has made His Master Plan available to you—He has invited you to use it to receive something better, a blessing to meet every need of your life. But if you make all kinds of excuses why you can't apply its truths and principles, you'll miss out on the benefits. If you delay by saying, "I'll give to God later when I can afford it more," or even, "I'll pay my obligations first and then I'll give," or even, "I'll give, but I sure don't expect anything in return"—your bid for success and prosperity will fail.

God is ready to bless you *now*, and if you will not allow Him to send *now* prosperity, He will find someone else He can bless. You know what it takes to activate the powerful force of God's Master Plan. And you know when you should do it—*right now!*

In the 118th Psalm, David recognized that God's blessings are for *now*. He gave you and me a Bible prayer to pray that can absolutely turn our lives around and enrich us beyond our fondest dreams. It's only eight words long—"O LORD, I BESEECH THEE, SEND NOW PROSPERITY" (v. 25).

David said, "Ask for prosperity. Ask for blessing. Ask for success." And do it now.

Send *now* prosperity

This is God's time to prosper you. This is the day for you to start receiving from God. Pray this simple Bible prayer—SEND *NOW* PROS— PERITY.

Are you ready for it? If you'll read the entire 118th Psalm, you'll notice that David first gave thanks to God. Then he reminded himself of all the blessings he had received already. And his heart was filled with praise to God. Then—and only then—David was ready to ask for prosperity.

I want you to follow the very same formula David did in Psalm 118. Give thanks for God's mercy that endures forever. Remind yourself of all the Lord's blessings you have received. Praise the Lord from the depths of your soul and being. Then you are ready to pray. It doesn't have to be a long or fancy prayer. And you don't have to beat around the bush, either. Just come right out and ask for what you need— "O Lord, I beseech thee, send now prosperity."

Notice that you're not asking for next week, next month, or next year. You're asking for *now*. And that's just how fast God's Master Plan can work for you. *Now!*

Oh, David had one more thing to say that is interesting and important. He said, "God is our light. I present to him my sacrifice" (v. 27, TLB). In other words, David said I didn't think this up by myself—it came from the inspiration of God. And I realize to receive the prosperity I want from God, I must first give to Him.

It all depends on you

You see, it all comes back to the principles of God's Master Plan. You must trust in God as your Supplier. You must put Him first in your life by giving. And then you can expect something better.

It all depends on what you do *now*.

Send now *prosperity*

Give God a chance to bless you today. Give Him the opportunity to answer your prayer for success and prosperity. Put Him first by giving to His Kingdom. Start praising Him as something better starts flowing into your life in a mighty river of blessing. Pray with me—"O Lord, I beseech thee, send *now* prosperity."

Important truths to remember:
1. God is pleased when you and your family are blessed and prospered. He wants you to have something better.
2. God loves everybody. What He does for one person, He will do for another. You can be just as blessed as anyone else in the whole world.
3. Giving is the engine that pulls a train-load of blessings. Vow and pay is the trigger that sets off an explosion of blessing.
4. There is no tomorrow in God's Master Plan. God wants to bless you *now*.
5. The most important prayer you can pray after you become a child of God is, "O Lord, I beseech thee, send *now* prosperity."

Send now *prosperity*

Give God a chance to bless you today. Give Him the opportunity to answer your prayer for success and prosperity. Put Him first by giving to His Kingdom. Start praising Him as something better starts flowing into your life in a mighty river of blessing. Pray with me—"O Lord, I beseech thee, send *now* prosperity."

Important truths to remember:
1. God is pleased when you and your family are blessed and prospered. He wants you to have something better.
2. God loves everybody. What He does for one person, He will do for another. You can be just as blessed as anyone else in the whole world.
3. Giving is the engine that pulls a train-load of blessings. Vow and pay is the trigger that sets off an explosion of blessing.
4. There is no tomorrow in God's Master Plan. God wants to bless you *now*.
5. The most important prayer you can pray after you become a child of God is, "O Lord, I beseech thee, send *now* prosperity."

149

13

Bible keys for Miracle Success

1. You were created in the image of God, filled with special God-like qualities.

> And God saw every thing that he had made, and, behold, it was very good. (Gen. 1:31)

You are God's special creation. You are a success waiting to unfold. God, in His infinite wisdom, has created you in His own image, after His own heart. He has endowed you with all the capabilities and abilities you need to become His child . . . successful in every thing you set your hand to do.

2. You are God's miracle of success for the world to see.

> For then thou shalt make thy way prosperous, and then thou shalt have good success. (Josh. 1:8)

Your successful life is a direct reflection on

God. When people see you have the upper hand in bad situations, that you know how to deal with temptation and defeat, and that your life is filled with more meaning and purpose, people see God in you. They see a miracle—a person filled with happiness and good success. YOU are God's miracle for the world to see.

3. God takes care of His own, and you are His.

The world is mine, and the fulness thereof. (Ps. 50:12)

With God as your Father, you don't have to worry about shortages and lack of resources. For He owns it all—everything. You are one of God's children. You can claim what you need from your Father. You are His child and He wants you to enjoy all He has provided. The old chorus says it best, "He owns the cattle on a thousand hills . . . and I know He takes care of me."

4. Let God release you from anger and bitterness with His Master Key called forgiveness.

And when ye stand praying, forgive, if ye have ought against any: that your Father also which is in heaven may forgive you your trespasses. (Mark 11:25)

152

Now, I know there are some people who have done you wrong, who may have caused you to stumble and fall, people it seems impossible to forgive and love. But remember this, God has something better for you when you release your anger. It is burning energy and causing you to miss out on the miracle success God has for you. Forgiveness—it is your key for today. Wipe the slate clean and let God handle your anger and hurt. He will do it.

5. We learn success secrets from studying our past failures and then moving ahead.

And the Lord said . . . Go forward. (Exod. 14:15)

Every day you can learn something more about yourself and the people around you. You can begin to understand why you act and feel like you do at times. Now, you and I aren't perfect, so we should ask God to teach us lessons through the mistakes we make. Then, we forget yesterday and its failures and move ahead.

6. Don't dwell on past failures and mistakes.

Behold, I will do a new thing; now it shall spring forth; shall ye not know it? I will even make a way in the wilderness, and rivers in the desert. (Isa. 43:19)

The past is behind you. Forget yesterday. Today, God has something better for you. God wants to raise you up, out of the ashes of defeat, and set your feet on steady ground. Learn all you can from past mistakes, but then move ahead. God has a better tomorrow for you.

7. Reaching out to others in need, planting positive seeds of love and encouragement, will put you a step ahead.

The liberal soul shall be made fat: and he that watereth shall be watered also himself. (Prov. 11:25)

Be an encourager to the discouraged. The principles of God's Master Plan work in every area of life. Be liberal with your love and concern. Be generous with patience and kindness. Those very things will return to you. As Solomon, the wisest man who ever lived, said . . . you are "watered yourself" when you reach out to help others.

8. Loneliness and aloneness are not the same.

As I was with Moses, so I will be with thee: I will not fail thee, nor forsake thee . . . . be not afraid, neither be thou dismayed: for the Lord thy God is with thee whithersoever thou goest. (Josh. 1:5, 9)

Realize you are never alone. When Moses died and Joshua was left with the awesome responsibility of leading the Israelites into Canaan, he knew what loneliness was. But then God came to Joshua and said, "I am always with you." Joshua was lonely but he found God was with him always, just as He is with you right now. You are never alone.

9. God's Master Plan for your life is beyond what you can possibly dream.

Now glory be to God who by his mighty power at work within us is able to do far more than we would ever dare to ask or even dream of—infinitely beyond our highest prayers, desires, thoughts, or hopes. (Eph. 3:20, TLB)

You and I can't begin to comprehend the greatness of God and His Master Plan. He has wonderful plans for you! You may wish you could have just a decent little house, when all the time God plans a beautiful palace for you. God's Master Plan for your success is beyond your wildest dreams.

10. The road to success is always under construction.

Commit thy way unto the Lord; trust also in him; and he shall bring it to pass. (Ps. 37:5)

Every experience that comes your way is going to help shape you as a person and help you mature into all God has in mind for you. God is continually molding us. He never gives up on us, although sometimes we seem to give up on Him. God wants you continually growing, reaching upward toward His something better.

11. God won't release you from all your problems, but He promises you success in dealing with your problems. And He will take you through the valley to something better.

For God hath caused me to be fruitful in the land of my affliction. (Gen. 41:52)

You and I still face problems every day. That's part of living in an imperfect world. God promises to take us through the valley—it is not a dead-end street. There is a way out and God will provide it. So don't stop short of the Promised Land. Keep moving. Keep believing. A better tomorrow is ahead for you. God can make every bad situation work for your good.

12. You can have the mind of God if you only ask for it.

And I have filled him with the spirit of God, in wisdom, and in understanding, and in knowledge, and in all manner of workmanship. (Exod. 31:3)

God promises to renew our inner man every day. (See 2 Cor. 4:16.) And when God is our partner, He actually transforms our mind and understanding into a miracle of wisdom and knowledge. Do you need more skill and ability today? Then ask God to fill you with Himself.

13. Success in any area of life requires discipline and hard work.

Study to shew thyself approved unto God, a workman that needeth not to be ashamed, rightly dividing the word of truth. (2 Tim. 2:15)

God does not approve of laziness. The key to confidence and ultimate success in any area of life is discipline. Discipline produces confidence, the confidence you need to become God's miracle of success for the world to see. Discipline yourself. Obey God. Do what He says.

14. Success comes in cans, not can'ts.

I can do all things through Christ which strengtheneth me. (Phil. 4:13)

Your attitude is all important. If you believe that with God all *is* possible, you'll be a winner. Continue to affirm His positive promises. Don't let the devil plant seeds of defeat and failure, an "I can't do it" attitude. God is with you, and you are becoming His miracle of success.

15. God's success for you is all inclusive.

Beloved, I wish above all things that thou mayest prosper and be in health, even as thy soul prospereth. (3 John 2)

If you have spiritual victory and freedom, but are still suffering and sick, you don't feel successful. And if you feel healthy, but are barely scraping by and have bill collectors knocking on your door, you don't feel like a success either.

So God's plan for you includes success in every area of your life. His kind of success is all inclusive. He wants you successful in spirit, in mind, in body, and in your finances. God cares about YOU and about every aspect of your personality and life that make you unique.

16. Don't give up!

Ask, and it shall be given you; seek, and ye shall find; knock, and it shall be opened unto you. (Matt. 7:7)

Someone once said the difference between success and failure is five minutes. Five more minutes of holding the rope. Five more minutes of trying harder. Five more minutes of not giving up. Don't give up on God. He never gives up on you! Keep holding on, just a little while longer. Even if the day looks dark and full of failures, remember that it is impossible to hold back the dawn. Ask, and *keep on* asking. Seek, and *keep on* seeking. Knock, and *keep on* knocking. You will receive.

17. Grace, God's love and favor, is a free gift to help you on the road to success.

Where sin abounded, grace did much more abound. (Rom. 5:20)

Actually, the dictionary says that grace is "unmerited divine assistance." That means an undeserved helping hand because of who you are. A child of the King. So quit struggling. Accept your inheritance—the great and miraculous grace of a God who loves you so much He gave and continues to give to you.

18. Keep planting seeds. Plant what you've got and harvest what you need.

Give, and it shall be given unto you. (Luke 6:38)

There are no shortcuts. If you want to receive something from God, you must first give something for Him to work with. He will take what you have and, by a miracle, use it to supply that miracle of success you need. The principles of sowing and reaping are as old as creation and nature itself . . . so keep planting seeds. God never stops giving to us. You and I must continually keep the pump primed to keep the blessings flowing.

19. Ask God for guidance when an important decision needs making.

If any of you lack wisdom, let him ask of God, that giveth to all men liberally, and upbraideth not; and it shall be given him. (James 1:5)

You may be facing a crisis today. You may need to make a decision that will affect your future or the future of a loved one. Sometimes it's like that. We're desperate with our back against the wall and are scared we'll make the wrong decision. After all, we are human, right? Yes, we're human. But we have God within us, beside us, behind us, before us. He *is* there. And He will fill you with a supernatural decision-making ability now.

20. Do your best—and let God handle the rest.

And having done all, to stand. (Eph. 6:13)

God expects you to do all you can to make your way prosperous. He has endowed you with ability and intelligence, with energy and purpose and goals. You can do your best for Him. But after you do all you can to conquer a problem, remember to relax and let God handle the rest. God is greater than any problem you will ever encounter. He will meet you at the point of your need with something better.

The Apostle Paul was very wise when he said, "do all you can, then stand." Stand up straight, with the confidence that you've done what you can and now God is going to handle the rest.

21. Take pride in the special job God has given you.

> You are not like that, for you have been chosen by God himself—you are priests of the King, you are holy and pure, you are God's very own—all this so that you may show to others how God called you out of the darkness into his wonderful light. (1 Pet. 2:9, TLB)

When God needs a job done, He almost always calls on one person to do it. So take pride in the assignment God has given you. You are unique. You are a one-of-a-kind original. You can do some things that no one else on earth can do as well as you. You are important and what you do is important.

22. Success begins with liking yourself.

Thou shalt love thy neighbor as thyself.
(Matt. 22:39)

See yourself as God sees you, rising out of the
slave mentality to live like a child of the King.
In order to love our neighbor, we first have to
love ourselves. That is one of the primary teachings of Jesus. Jesus knew that a healthy self-love
is necessary in order to achieve miracle success.
You are a person worth loving! By faith, begin
to see yourself as the person God wants you to
be. Visualize yourself becoming what God said
you could be. You are a person of worth and
value.

God doesn't see what you have been as much
as He sees what you are going to be. He sees all
your good qualities and positive attributes. God
loves you—and you should too.

23. You have unlimited potential.

For with God nothing shall be impossible.
(Luke 1:37)

You hold the seeds to success in your hands.
Prosperity is well within your reach. You're
like the miner who unknowingly sat on the
largest gold mine right in his own back yard.
You have the key to success within your reach,
for the Kingdom of God is *within you*. Together with

God, you can turn any problem, any mountain into a miracle. Look around you. Do you see what I see? I see you rising up out of sin, sickness and poverty. I see you coming out of depression and oppression. With God as your partner, you are guaranteed unlimited success.

24. You should have definite goals in mind, a plan for achieving miracle success.

I am the Lord thy God which teacheth thee to profit, which leadeth thee by the way that thou shouldest go. (Isa. 48:17)

What would it take for you to feel successful? What achievements do you look forward to being blessed with? In order to know God's miracle success, you must firmly implant in your mind your goals and plans. Set a goal for each day, for each week. Then as you achieve these goals with God's help, you'll be making your way up the path to miracle success. God will teach you how to profit, which path to take, and what goals you should set for yourself.

25. Always look up instead of letting a bad situation always drag you down.

I will lift up mine eyes unto the hills, from whence cometh my help. (Ps. 121:1)

Look up, above your problems. Look up,

there's a new day coming for you. Look up, God is greater than the bad situation that is dragging you down. Look up, you can't hold back the dawn of something better.

When you look up, you'll find Jesus. He's there—above the bad circumstances, above the pain and suffering, above the worry and fear. Look up and find His miracle touch of love.

26. Let God tame the fear and worry in your life. These are real barriers to achieving success.

I sought the Lord, and He heard me, and delivered me from all my fears. (Ps. 34:4)

When the disciples found themselves caught in a fierce storm at sea, they were so overcome with fear and worry they temporarily forgot about Jesus. They spent all their energies focusing on their problem. They didn't give Jesus a chance to focus their minds on a solution. Then Jesus came, and calmed the troubled waters. Today, Jesus is calming the storms in your life.

He is with you, to tame the fear and worry that burns so much of your energy. God hasn't given you a spirit of fear, but of power and of love and a sound mind. (See 2 Tim. 1:7.)

27. The truth will set you free.

And ye shall know the truth, and the truth shall make you free. (John 8:32)

Famous philosophers and psychologists have
been looking for the answer to ultimate success
and joy for centuries, and much has been written about finding eternal happiness. But this
one verse in the New Testament sums up everything that is important to your achieving miracle success. The truth *will* set you free. The
liberating truth is that God *is* Who He says He
is. He has a Master Plan for you, a plan for good.
He has a purpose for your life, a way for you to
achieve lasting success. And He promises to
never, never leave you. That truth sets you free
and will continue to set you free from every
doubt and worry if you'll claim it right now.

28. God's healing promises are for you!

He giveth power to the faint; and to them
that have no might he increaseth strength.
(Isa. 40:29)

The Bible is filled with positive promises for
healing. It is God's Master Plan that you be
healthy and wealthy in every area of your life.
So often, we may read these promises in the
Bible and then say to ourselves, "Oh, that means
somebody else. I guess I am just destined to
suffer." That is the devil planting negative
seeds in your mind. Don't let him do it! Study
your Bible. Commit to memory the healing pas-
sages in the Bible. Then claim those promises

and continue to claim them for your healing.
God does have health and strength for you.

29. Exercise common sense and discipline in the areas of exercise and proper eating habits.

They that seek the Lord shall not want any
good thing. (Ps. 34:10)

Check yourself to be sure you are not contributing to your illness through bad habits, wrong
diet, or not enough exercise and rest. When a
person says he wants to be healed, yet knowingly abuses his body, it's hard to believe he
is sincere. Even if he does get healed, his sins
against God's laws of nature may bring sickness
to him again.

30. Courage is not the absence of fear.

Be strong and of a good courage, fear not,
nor be afraid of them: for the Lord thy God,
he it is that doth go with thee; he will not
fail thee, nor forsake thee. (Deut. 31:6)

Courage is the ability to move ahead, with
God's power, in spite of fear. Then when you
take that first and hardest step, God will step in
to deliver you from fear. He continually fills
you with the courage you need to face what lies
ahead. Courage is God-given. Only He can give

you strength to move ahead even when the going
gets rough. He is with you, in every endeavor, in
every crisis. He is leading you toward a moun-
tain-moving miracle.

31. Claim miracle success in your life today because it is God's plan for you.

For I know the plans I have for you, says
the Lord. They are plans for good and not
for evil, to give you a future and a hope.
(Jer. 29:11, TLB)

Miracle success is for you! You have a bright
future and an unlimited opportunity, because
God's plans for you are for your good. When
you incorporate this great Bible truth into your
whole being and claim it for your life, you've
begun your life of miracle success. God's blessings on you. You have better tomorrows ahead.

God's Master Plan

God's Master Plan will work for you because it's 100% Bible.

Read these scriptures until you know each one. They contain the Bible keys to success. These principles will change your life when you do your part.

Phil. 4:19	Matt. 7:7-8
Luke 6:38	James 4:2
Mark 11:24	Ps. 50:12
3 John 2	2 Cor. 9:6
Josh. 1:7-8	Prov. 11:24-25
Hag. 2:8	Heb. 6:14
Deut. 28:2	Deut. 29:9
Deut. 8:18	2 Chron. 26:5
Matt. 7:11	Mal. 3:10
Ps. 35:27	Matt. 6:31-33
Luke 12:32	Ps. 118:25

Here's what you do to make God's Master Plan work.

You can be a winner!

You can have success and happiness—financially, physically and spiritually.

Why? Because it's God's will for you. The Bible says, "Beloved, I wish above all things that thou mayest prosper and be in health, even as thy soul prospereth" (3 John 2).

How? By following the simple principles of God's Master Plan that are bringing blessings to thousands. No matter what your need, these three simple steps can help bring you victory.

1. Trust God as your Supplier.

This is the secret. "But my God shall supply all your need according to his riches in glory by Christ Jesus" (Phil. 4:19).

2. Give and it shall be given unto you.

Putting God first through your giving must be a regular part of your life. "Give, and it shall be given unto you; good measure, pressed down, and shaken together, and running over, shall men give into your bosom. For with the same measure that ye mete withal it shall be measured to you again" (Luke 6:38).

3. Expect God to provide something better.

When you give God your best you can ask God

for His best and expect to receive it. "Therefore I say unto you, What things soever ye desire, when ye pray, believe that ye receive them, and ye shall have them" (Mark 11:24).

The Miracle Prayer Garden is the very heart of the Don Stewart ministry. Dedicated prayer partners are on duty to take your call and pray for you 24 hours a day.

The Miracle Prayer Garden offers light in the darkest hour, faith and encouragement when all hope is gone, a spiritual shelter in the time of storm.

When you need prayer, the Miracle Prayer Garden is as close as your telephone. No matter how desperate your need may be, help is available. Is anything too hard for God? Jesus said, "Ask what ye will, and it shall be done unto you" (John 15:7). Don Stewart and his prayer partners are waiting to believe with you now.

DON STEWART'S
WORLDWIDE OUTREACHES
MISSIONS • CRUSADES • TELEVISION
LITERATURE • BIBLE TRAINING

Miracle Prayer Garden
For prayer help call (602) 995-HELP